Memories ui

Befreite Erinn

German Children in World War II

Deutsche Kinder im Zweiten Weltkrieg

edited by

Barbara Ottaway und Renate Mehta

Exeter/Berlin 2015

For our children and children's children
in the hope
that they will never have to live through a war

Für unsere Kinder und Kindeskinder
in der Hoffnung,
dass sie nie einen Krieg erleben müssen

To Joyce & Brian
with my best wishes
from Barbara

Content - Inhalt

FOREWORD

Memories of my childhood during the Second World War in Germany had been floating around in my head for several decades: sentences – short paragraphs – unconnected incidents – memories awakened by watching documentaries and films of the Second World War – but memories which had never been openly acknowledged or written down. I found that the same had happened to the friends from my student days in Berlin, even though we never talked about our memories then or at our later, irregular meetings. We had all concentrated on forgetting about the terrible war and post-war years: passing examinations, finding jobs, getting married, having families ....

The recent horror of women and children fleeing from yet another war, at first in Syria and now spreading to most of the Levant and the Middle East, vividly brought back my own memories and prompted me to start writing them down. My co-editor and I started to collect the stories of our fellow college students from our Berlin student days in the late 1950s. Of the college year graduating in 1958, only nine of us are still alive. We now want to put these memories on paper while we still can.

The text consists of 13 stories of the war and post-war years, written by women born in Germany, and the stories of some of their friends and husbands, all but one born between 1937 and 1939.

They tell of their childhood spent in Berlin and many diverse parts of what was then Germany; of bombed-out cities; of coming under direct attack by low-flying fighter planes; of spending numerous nights in cramped cellars during bombardments; of fleeing just in front of the approaching Soviet army with the thunderous noise of cannons shaking the ground beneath; of ending up near Dresden, just before that awful night of the bombing and the fire storm; of narrowly missing boarding the ill-fated vessel *Gustloff*, which sank in the Baltic packed with refugees, and of ending up in a Danish camp behind barbed wire for two years after the end of the war.

Some of us had been evacuated into the Eastern provinces during the war. Almost all of us became refugees, leaving most or all of our possessions behind, either fleeing from the Eastern provinces towards the end of the war, or illegally crossing from Russian-occupied East Germany into West Germany after the war. This led to many of us ending up in very cramped accommodation indeed, mostly in towns where we did not know anyone. To compound this situation, there did not seem to have been any voluntary organisations caring for refugees, as would have happened in the UK, collecting second-hand clothing, shoes or household items.

As told in the memories, some childhoods were spent in peaceful surroundings and described an almost idyllic life with extended families nearby with the war a distant happening. But all too soon the effects of war were encroaching, bombed-out people from big towns were coming to the countryside with horror stories to tell, news of defeats at the front were filtering through to the population, news came of the death of fathers, sons and relatives. Towards the end of the war and in post-war years hunger, fear and a sense of anxiety were always present in most of us, even though many of the adults around us tried to hide their anxieties. Some stories are interspersed with crazy, dangerous post-war adventures but also with war-time recipes and tales of growing vegetables and flowers amongst the ruins. All of us are forever grateful to our mothers who showed such strength, ingenuity and unselfish care to make life as normal as possible for us in utterly chaotic surroundings and conditions. It is to our mothers that we would like to dedicate this volume.

None of the authors of the 13 stories are professional writers of prose. What is noticeable, and certainly was never discussed amongst us before writing our pieces, is the non-emotional, non-dramatic style in which we wrote. Indeed, we instinctively found that it was the only style which allowed us to deal with the memories. It has been a long emotional journey – several of us almost gave up writing, overcome by memories which had taken so long to forget.

The stories collected here show that sheer survival, finding shelter and food was foremost in most people's minds during and directly after the war, as was a kind of dogged persistence to carry on living and to stay in contact with the remaining members of their families. Perhaps this is the reason why most of the stories are told in an unemotional, factual style.

We were small children during the Second World War, so naturally we only knew our own pain and anxieties. In the 1950s, in our teens, when we learned about the crimes and atrocities of Nazi Germany, of our own people, these discoveries added another level of horror and shame to our childhood experiences. Like most Germans, we brought a mental iron curtain down to enable us to get on with our lives. Some people even now are unable to unlock their wartime memories.

Over the last few years, several newspaper articles, radio and TV programmes and books on the generation of WWII children, the *Kriegskinder*, have come out both in Germany and also in Austria. Journalist and author Sabine Bode, for instance, has collected many first-hand stories from that generation and written, already in 2004, a thought-provoking book, *Die vergessene Generation: Die Kriegskinder brechen ihr Schweigen* (*The forgotten generation: WWII children break their silence*). Interviewees would question her motives, asking 'Do you want to portray the Germans as victims?' or 'Are you implying I am traumatised?' Early on in her project, she found that her articles or scripts for TV programmes were repeatedly ignored and forgotten, and concluded that the weight of guilt and shame about the crimes of the Nazi era had buried the *Kriegskinder*'s memories. Now there are seminars, meetings and publications in Germany, and often this is the first time the *Kriegskinder* talk about their experiences – seven decades after the events.

The maps accompanying each of the memories show that the majority of us came from the north-eastern parts of what was then Germany. This is largely explained by the fact that we had met in Berlin to study. Furthermore, many were born in areas which were later to be occupied by the Russian Allies. It is possible therefore that the number of us who had to flee or wanted to cross over into the zones occupied by the Western Allies, is higher than in the rest of Germany. For instance, our only Bavarian author's story tells of a much less dramatic wartime experience. Nevertheless, judging by German and Austrian publications, experiences throughout these two countries have been similar. Together, they form a pattern of destruction, deprivation and suffering which are the terrible effects of war which we now have to watch unfold again all over the Middle East.

Economic collapse, dictatorship, propaganda and the overall chaos caused by armed conflict must provide us with the context in which these individual histories took place.

One thought that unites us is the absolute aversion to war and armed conflict. We are not sentimental, let alone proud about

Germany's past and certainly we do not see ourselves as victims; on the contrary, we still find it incomprehensible and shameful that our parents' generation could not or would not stop Hitler in time to prevent the unimaginable horrors inflicted on fellow-citizens and neighbouring countries. We are deeply moved by the plight of the many civilians, mostly women and children, who suffer from the effects of war, armed brutalities and post-war deprivation, regardless of whether they are on the winner's or the loser's side.

Barbara Ottaway, 2014

A few notes by the translator

The individual memories have been closely translated by one of us from their original German into English. A few terms may not be very familiar to readers not from Germany and, although some have already been explained in the memories themselves, **always bracketed and in** *italic,* some more detail is given here.

Age of children starting school in Germany was, and still is, on or around the sixth birthday.

De-Nazification: A programme initiated by the Allies after the war to rid Germans and Austrians, particularly those who had been members of the NSDAP, the National Socialist German Workers' Party, of any remnants of Nazi ideology.

Kinderlandverschickung (KLV): During the war, Hitler sent 14-year-old boys to camps, where they would be indoctrinated with Nazi ideology, embedded in activities and sport.

Maids: Hitler wanted to encourage women to have as many children as possible during the war. For this reason he started a programme of *Pflichtjahrmädchen*, 'mother's helps'   or 'housemaids'. They were 14-year-old girls, who, after eight years of schooling, came to help families with new babies and with general household duties. Most, but not all, lived with the families.

Volkssturm: A bit like Britain's 'Dad's Army', this consisted of old men and, towards the end of the war, also 15-year-old boys trained briefly in the KLV camps. They had to dig last-minute defences and ditches in roads, man air-defence positions, etc.

Maps: There are thirteen maps, one for each memory. They are placed between the English and the German texts. Clear explanations in German are on the maps themselves. For the English reader there is an explanatory page preceding the maps.

Anne's Memories

I was born on the 25th of August 1935 in Berlin's district of Dahlem (see map 1 for main places mentioned in text) and I have no sisters or brothers. My mother, who was sure at a later time that Hitler meant war, had already packed large suitcases with things that could be packed early, like blankets and bed linen, when the bombardments started. It was my job to take a little suitcase full of our silver into the cellar when the sirens went. We had had the cellar in our house strengthened with some supporting beams. My mother had moved the cot I had as a small child into the cellar and put me into it every time we had to go down there.

At the beginning of 1943 the bombs fell onto our house. One of the mines exploded nearby and blew the roof tiles off the houses, allowing the incendiary bombs to fall directly into the houses. This caused a great wave of pressure which made me fly out of my bed straight into the arms of my mother who was standing in front of the cot. The tremendous noise from outside of booming planes, of anti-aircraft cannons firing and of the rustling noise of falling bombs is still in my ears today. The few men who were still with us, including my father, rushed out of the cellar and found our house in flames. They tried to extinguish the fires but it was a hopeless undertaking. My mother rescued what she could: as we lived on the ground floor she simply threw everything she could reach out of the window, including the cases that were already packed, and in this way we were able to save many belongings. All these rescued things, together with those from other burnt-out houses, stood on the street for several days but nothing was stolen.

I was seven at the time and while all the houses around us where going up in flames I sat with nanny in a little garden hut opposite our house. I lived through the terrifying firestorm which developed after a while and which sent out flames in all directions. Finally, the crashing collapse of the roof left an impression which I have not forgotten to this day.

I cannot remember how many days I stayed on in Berlin after the loss of our house. We stayed with various friends until an uncle arranged for me to go to the estate of his brother and sister, cousins of my mother, in Marienmünster in Westphalia. My parents took me there by train and by bus and then returned to Berlin. For me the war was forgotten: I enjoyed my childhood surrounded by cows, pigs, chickens and especially by horses to which I became passionately attached. I grew up healthy in body and soul and without trauma. Or so I thought....

Then I found the following short account which my aunt had written about the time when I was living at her place and which she gave to me at my wedding:

Anne was deeply worried and unhappy when she heard at school that Berlin had been bombarded again. The children at school were very keen to tell her of the things which we had anxiously tried to keep from her. I found out that Anne was afraid for her own life when we had a violent thunderstorm, during which one lightning bolt after another fell on the forest and one clap of thunder followed another while we calmly watched the spectacle. Anne, the little city girl, had never experienced such a thunderstorm and thought it was a bombardment of which we backwoodsmen had no idea. She shouted "To the cellar, to the cellar!" It was hard to make her believe that she was experiencing a natural phenomenon.

This story shows that I had by no means forgotten the war and may also explain the next two memories which had lain dormant:

Much later, when I was married and expecting my first child, we lived in Arnhem, in Holland, in an apartment on the third floor. The apartment was beautiful, roomy and had two balconies. However, as soon as I became pregnant I had the same dream every night: sirens raising the alarm, booming planes, falling bombs. I crept on my stomach through a small hole in the earth into a kind of bunker, full of people – a feeling of claustrophobia came over me. As soon as I woke, the dream was gone and forgotten. But the next night it came back again. When Andries was born the dream disappeared.

Then I became pregnant again. The dream came back – every night. Why? Then it came to me: because of the responsibility for the new life I probably felt shut in, not free or in control in this apartment. There was no possibility of avoiding danger or running away, for instance into a wood. Also there was no garden where I could grow food to feed us. When I was in my third month we were able to buy a house in a leafy area, surrounded by a garden and about 200 metres away from a wood. Immediately the dreams stopped.

I have never again dreamt of war.

Barbara's Memories

I was born in Dresden (see map 2 for main places mentioned in text) a year before World War II started. I went back about 20 years ago and found the block of houses in which my parents had an apartment still standing, surrounded by green parkland. These houses had been in a side street off a busy main road before the war, but nothing apart from this group of houses was left standing after the massive fire-bombing of Dresden. Another visit in 2012 and re-building had taken place – very little of the green parkland was left.

My mother had become very frightened by the bombing raids which had destroyed big towns such as Hamburg, Berlin, Leipzig, and Kassel. In late 1943 she moved with us three children, my two younger brothers and me, to her parents' in Annaberg, while my father was fighting in the war on many different frontlines. The town of Annaberg lies in the Erzgebirge, the ore mountains, close to the Czech border. My grandparents had an apartment in their tall house near the central market-place. It was on the first floor and had a wonderful stove, one of those tiled stoves where you could sit on a bench, which ran all the way round it, and warm yourself in the winter. My grandparents' textiles shop was on the ground floor and ran the whole depth of the building to the back yard. We children were not often allowed to explore it, but loved it when we could, because it was full of bales of the most gorgeous materials, many differently coloured threads and buttons of all shapes and colours. Every apartment in the house had a section of the cellar as well as a section of the attic above the fourth floor, for drying clothes, and a non-flushing toilet half-way up the main staircase shared with the people living one floor up.

Soon after we moved to Annaberg, the air- raids started. I still can't hear a siren going off without remembering that time. When the air-raids became more frequent, I had to get my brothers dressed in a hurry, while my mother helped my grandparents to get ready. We all had to go down to the cellar and await the All-Clear siren. Mostly, we would be there for a long time in this confined space. Sometimes, my uncle, who had fought in the First World War, and occasionally stayed with us, would take me up the stairs to watch the planes flying above us, dropping their bombs. But because Annaberg was on a mountain the bombs would almost always drift off, not hitting their target, Annaberg, but the next town of Buchholz. That town was almost completely destroyed.

Most air-raids seem to have been at night. However, there was one I remember which was during the afternoon when my mother had taken us to my grandparents' garden by the town wall. When the sirens went we tried to get back to the house, about a quarter of an hour away, but got caught by the town wall. We pressed ourselves against it when the first wave of fighter planes flew over us. When this wave was over, a warden in black uniform, who had also been caught there, told us to hide quickly under the bushes on the other side of the footpath and to cover up my bright red dress. So my mother threw her coat over me and we cowered there not daring to look up at the fighter planes going over us. They seemed to be so close that we imagined seeing the pilots' heads in the cockpits when we did peep. Whether that is true or imagined I cannot tell. After the All-Clear we collected the spent cartridges along the path.

My father was wounded twice, once in the Crimea and the second time in Russia. After the second time he was sent home from the front to recover. I remember it was in the winter and there was deep snow on all the roads. He took me out tobogganing and I probably got too cold and screamed until I was blue in the face. This first amused, then frightened him and we went home quickly. He did not talk much to us about the war either then or later – it must have been too awful.

The end of the war is deeply embedded in my memory: there had been a stream of refugees coming through Annaberg for weeks: families with handcarts, prams, anything that had wheels, packed with belongings and children. Mixed with this stream of refugees were now army vehicles. Then, this stream suddenly stopped and there was an eerie silence for half an hour or so. Suddenly an endless line of menacing-looking Russian tanks rolled through the town, along the street where my grandparents' house was. We children wanted to open the windows and perhaps catch one of the sweets the soldiers were throwing to the children. However, we were not allowed to and were told that the sweets were sure to be poisoned!

Plundering, theft, rape and general chaos followed and my mother decided to flee for a little while with us children, her sister and our uncle to a neighbouring village. With two prams we walked for several hours through the woods. The adults probably made it sound like an adventure for I cannot remember that any sinister thoughts crossed my mind.

After some weeks we returned to Annaberg. Life became harder for us all. There was little food and every kind of butter, oil and fat had run out. The same piece of bacon rind was used again and again to grease the frying pan to fry potato skins. My grandparents had their textiles shop confiscated and in retrospect I realise that my grandfather lost his mind around that time. So it was left to my mother and grandmother to fend for us and feed us all. They also had to hide the bread from my grandfather whom they discovered sometimes helping himself to more than his one slice a day. Luckily the garden provided a lot of vegetables and fruit and, importantly for the adults, tobacco. My mother, like most women then, was a very inventive cook: we ate nettle soup, for instance, and did not complain. We also collected a lot of rosehips and elderberries which were turned into juice and bottled or made into jam. To this day I cannot bear to eat anything made with rosehips or elderberries, but no doubt this is one of the reasons why we all grew up relatively healthy. However, my little brother did contract diphtheria. He was running a very high temperature, shaking his little cot, trying to get out of it; and as there were no antibiotics, his recovery was a close-run thing.

My mother started a small business organising the distribution of yarn to a group of women who knitted baby clothes with it. These she would take out to the country and exchange them for butter, flour and anything edible she could get hold of. Then this small, indomitable woman would carry it all back on overloaded trains and give a share to the women in lieu of payment; the rest was for payment for the yarn and for us. Most of the adults at that time smoked and we grew our own tobacco in the garden by the town wall. When the leaves were harvested we helped to string them up, and hang them up to dry in the attic. When they were ready the leaves were rolled up and cut.

'Who is that man?' asked my little brother as my mother dropped him into the small zinc bath: my father had just walked into the courtyard many months after the end of the war, during which time we had heard nothing of him and did not know whether he was alive or dead. It was in the autumn of 1946 and I had escorted my father to my aunt's house at the edge of a village where my mother had gone with my two little brothers. I had stayed behind with my grandparents in Annaberg because I had to go to school. My father had just been released from a prisoner-of-war camp in Poland, having been a prisoner-of-war before that in a Russian camp. He had pretended that his family was in West Germany as he was aware that in the East German zone, occupied by the Russians, all men - and particularly all engineers - were taken straight back to Siberia upon release, to rebuild all the machinery and factories the Russians had taken from Germany to Siberia after the end of the war. He had risked recapture by coming over to see us. My grandparents thought it was safer for him if he travelled with me to my aunt's house to be reunited with the rest of the family.

After a short time my father went back to 'the West', first to the north of Germany, to find work in his profession as a civil engineer, and to find a place for us to live in. He later joined a small building firm in Schwelm, near Wuppertal in Westphalia, a town which had hardly been hit by bombing. I don't know how he let us know that we should come over to West Germany. We had to get from East to West Germany, across a border which was at that time patrolled by Russian soldiers. Somehow my mother managed to find local people who told her where to cross (through a forest) and when it was safe to cross (between Russian patrols). I cannot remember anything of that journey, other than that it was of paramount importance to be absolutely silent.

Finally in September 1947 we got to our new 'home'. The town officials in Schwelm had allocated one room in a couple's apartment to my father, his sister, who had joined him after fleeing from Silesia, and us four. One can imagine that the couple was not best pleased to have to take us in. The one room luckily had a balcony. My ever-resourceful mother got a barrel of 'Sauerkraut' going, as this was the cheapest food one could get. But the landlady, who had lost nothing during the war, complained of the smell. After a while my parents found a small attic room for my aunt and me and the single room became a bit less crowded.

I had to go to the local school, which was torture as I was teased mercilessly about my Saxon accent, which I admit is not exactly beautiful, and because I was always wearing the same clothes! Things improved a bit when I became friends with another girl, Christa. She always sat in the back row and cried a lot. I only later found out that the reason for this was that they had moved from the French-occupied zone to British-occupied Schwelm. Each zone had at this time different school-books and Christa was too afraid to tell her mother that she needed new books, an expense they could ill afford. Did the teachers not notice? We are still very good friends and only recently did she tell me that they were refugees, who had been close to Dresden during the awful bombing of that town.

My father was eventually allowed to rebuild the top floor of one of the few houses that had been bombed with the promise that we could rent that top-floor apartment. In the end the owner of the house went back on his word and we only got half the apartment. Nevertheless, with three small rooms and a kitchen, it was a great improvement even though we had to share the only bathroom with another family. However, we had absolutely no furniture and no money to buy any. What astonishes me now is that there was no organisation collecting surplus or second-hand clothing, furniture and household equipment for refugees, particularly for those with growing children.

My parents decided to try and get their furniture and belongings from East Germany. They put us into an orphanage in Bad Salzdetfurth, near Hanover, thinking that I would be able to look after my two little brothers. They did not reckon with the harsh rules of the orphanage, which immediately separated us. We were kept clean by daily baths in cold saltwater and the only time I could meet my little brothers was when we all went on our daily walks. I shall always remember how we walked, barefoot, but at least all together for a short time. We all had pot bellies from the watery soups we were given. My parents came back at last, having survived countless obstacles and dangerous situations during which they lost half their belongings as bribes to transport firms, train operators and Russian soldiers.

Slowly things improved: my parents managed to get an allotment where we could grow vegetables and even some strawberries and not every pair of outgrown shoes turned into a crisis. Our accents improved, we collected sacks full of beech nuts and exchanged them for oil, and we kept rabbits, which were meant to provide our Christmas dinner. But we children vetoed this plan and they survived – for a while. Then one escaped, or maybe it was stolen? At any rate, a little later we had some meat for supper! In 1952 my brother Christian was visiting relatives in Leipzig, in Russian-occupied Germany. He contracted scarlet fever and was in quarantine for several weeks. Eventually, my parents were able to send over penicillin and he was cured and could finally return to us.

At school our curriculum was rather patchy – for instance, history took us up to Napoleon but no further. There were few teachers who could be trusted with our education - so there has been a lot to catch up with.

In 1956 when I went to Berlin to study at a technical college, the city had been divided into zones occupied by the four Allies. At college we had fellow students who lived in the Russian-occupied zone. They were at that time still allowed to come over on a daily basis to the college which was in the zone occupied by the Western Allies. One of the girls improved her financial situation, thanks to the low exchange rate of East-to-West German currency, by smuggling over Jenaer glass *(pyrex glass produced in the East German town of Jena)* and selling it to us for less than the college would charge us for breakages in the laboratory. We Westerners, on the other hand, were able to afford occasional visits to East Berlin, the Brecht Theatre or even the Opera. How unfair was that?

In the college holidays I took the train home to my family, along the corridor from West Berlin, through the Russian-occupied zone of East Germany to West Germany. The trains were always locked so that no one could get on. At the border near Helmstedt, everyone had to get off and there would be a very thorough search of luggage, the carriages, the people and their papers by DDR guards and sometimes by Russian soldiers. Frequently, there were people who were not allowed to board the train again. Who knows what happened to them?

After this sinister part of the journey it was a double pleasure to arrive in Koblenz, where my family had moved in 1956. In the evenings our talks would frequently turn to the war – my brothers were then preparing for their 'Abitur' *(A-levels)*. As a student my father had joined a fencing students' corporation. These students' corporations had been transferred in their entirety into the Nazi Party and he went to war as a first lieutenant. We could not understand why he had joined such a corporation and, moreover, and naively, why he had not left it at the stage when it was transferred. We accused and bombarded our parents with questions about why Germany had been allowed to slip down this awful slope towards war and destruction and why nobody had been able to stop Hitler and the persecution and destruction of Jews. Even several years later, when my brother was studying in Berlin, these discussions continued on his visits home and once became so heated that he did not return for more than a year. Now, I feel sad that by verbally attacking our parents in this way we barred the way to finding out more about their personal experiences during the war. There were no easy answers to these questions then and to me there are still not enough answers to explain this dark chapter in history.

Bärbel's Memories

I was born in Berlin (see map 3 for main places mentioned in text) in October 1937, as my parents' third child. Their fourth, my youngest brother, was born in 1941. Relatives from Rio de Janeiro, cousins of my mother, were supposed to come to his christening ceremony but since the war had broken out in 1939 the christening took place two years later without them in our Markuskirche. A few months later, the church, which was only a few metres away from our home, was badly damaged in a bombing raid. The air-raids were steadily increasing and we often had to go into our air-raid shelter, where I was very afraid.

In 1943 families with many children were ordered to leave Berlin and my mother, with us four children, was evacuated to Bartenstein in East Prussia, south of Königsberg. We were sent to a beautiful estate with meadows, fields and forests, gabbling geese and plenty of milk, bread, potatoes, wonderful homemade ice cream and no air-raids. I was very happy there. Once, I was allowed to climb into the reconnaissance plane of the landlady's son, who was visiting his mother. My little brother and I were thrilled to be sitting in the cockpit, being envied by the village youths. Sadly, later, as a fighter pilot, the landlady's son was shot down. Despite its use for combat and bombing in wars, I still think that the aeroplane is one of mankind's greatest inventions.

Even today I can see myself standing at the window next to the landowner's wife and feeding mashed boiled potatoes to the gabbling geese below. In reality, I was afraid of these geese when I had to pass them in the morning on the way to school because they chased me, honking loudly.

13

After about two months we left East Prussia and spent the time up to our escape, in the middle of January 1945, in the town of Posen. We stayed there with my parents' friends from their student days who owned a large nursery. We called them Aunt Lisa and Uncle Dieter and they had two boys, aged five and eight years. Uncle Dieter was stationed at the front in Narvik in Norway. That is why Aunt Lisa had to manage the entire business by herself.

Posen was close enough to Berlin for my father to be able to visit us from time to time. He had already fought in WWI, but in 1944 he was nevertheless called up to join the army. He had to fight in various places, finally ending up on the Eastern Front in Pressburg (Bratislava, in Slovakia). We received a last message from him around Easter time, dated the 30th March 1945. He was presumed missing after that date. Until 1953, for eight long years, I hoped for his return and followed every radio announcement that gave lists of prisoners-of-war who had been released. After this time the Russian government insisted that there were no more prisoner-of-war camps. All my fantasies of travelling to Russia during my school holidays to search for my father, were now over - I had to accept his death.

In Posen I had a relatively easy time: there were no air-raids except for one on the middle of the town, where the main railway station and all our furniture, which my father had sent on to us, went up in flames. What irony!

I enjoyed the time in Posen. The workmen took me along to the fields on their horse-drawn carts. I prattled in their Polish language. I was cheerful at school and keen to learn, but hated the so-called 'Hitler Gruss' – right arm up, shouting 'Heil Hitler' – and that at the age of six!

Then, shortly after Christmas 1944, and rather unexpectedly, came the order to flee. My mother collected my elder brother, who had been sent home during the night from the KLV- camp (*a Hitler youth camp in the country, to which young boys were sent*). They arrived just in time and we set off in a temperature of minus 20 degrees on frozen roads in our open horse-drawn cart, drawn by our steady, brown horse, Hans, and the black horse, Vinzenz. There were six of us children, aged between three-and-a-half and ten, my mother, Aunt Lisa and the Polish coachman, who brought us safely to Bärwalde, just near the River Oder. Fortunately, he also got back again to Posen.

Just behind us rolled the Russian tanks; I thought it was the rumbling of a thunderstorm. The main tarmac roads were reserved for our army, rolling towards Berlin. Our route had to take the narrow roads through woods and villages. I thought it was a great adventure and we older children had a special task: we ran along beside the horse-drawn carts and threw stones under the back wheels so that they did not slip into the ditches beside the roads. This diverted my attention so that I didn't notice the terrible things that happened to others. We also did not suffer any chilblains on our hands and feet as others did. At night we would find shelter in villages or in deserted farmhouses. Once we stayed in a mill, where the miller and his wife looked after us although they themselves did not want to escape with us.

Aunt Lisa and her two children stayed in Bärwalde with her parents, but we went on straight away, carrying the few things

15

that we could carry in our hands. My little brother, for instance, carried the small milk can. We caught the train which took us over the River Oder to Berlin. A few hours later this bridge was blown up by the retreating German army.

Arriving back in Berlin, we were fortunate to find our house still standing. However, there were already two couples in it whose flats had been bombed. Another three lodgers joined us so that many people lived in our four-and-a-half-roomed flat. These crowded conditions continued until 1952. During the last few months of the war we experienced many terrible air-raids – we more or less lived in our air-raid shelters for four weeks. If we had gone outside, the low-flying fighter planes would have shot at us like rabbits. Even now, I cannot bear the penetrating sound of a siren and it took many years before I dared to go down into a cellar by myself. Although I find fireworks beautiful, I still jump terribly when the bang comes. At some stage a Russian soldier appeared in our cellar and we realised that Berlin-Steglitz was in Russian hands!

The post-war years were marked by cold, hunger and darkness. Around us there were the ruins in which we climbed about. These buildings were rebuilt only in 1959; I have been living in one of them for the past nine years. Again and again I find it inconceivable that we have lived through such times and wonder how we survived at all: often there was no water, no light and only rarely gas for the oven, and hardly anything to eat. First the Russian troops marched in, then the southern part of Berlin became the American zone. But still the rations we were able to obtain with our ration cards left us starving.

The mutual support amongst the adults was inspiring. The weirdest recipes were exchanged, for instance how to make a cake from coffee grounds, to bake biscuits from carrot peelings. That demonstrates what everyday life was like. The Americans provided meals for schools; my youngest brother, who was under school age, received special food from Sweden and cod-liver oil.

I even got my first chocolate from a Russian soldier, who saw my mother and us four children clambering about the piles of ruins. This reduced a little the fear of Russian soldiers which we had, due to our experience shortly after the end of the war, when the door bell had often rung and Russian soldiers had tried to search our flat always saying the same thing: 'Pistol, pistol, soldier, soldier, watches, watches.' The same thing happened at the beginning of the occupation to adults on the streets and they had to raise their arms as well. Our anxiety ran deep but we played in the ruins all the same. In a front garden of one of the ruined houses my mother grew vegetables, potatoes, tomatoes and also flowers. We carried the water for the plants up from the canal. Our toys, our beloved teddy bears, had stayed behind in Posen, but we received donations from the district council, often from America. For a long time we played with dice from America and France.

Once again the 'Berlin Blockade' by the Russians from 1948 to 1949 was terrible, because again we were close to starvation and freezing. Even now I am grateful to the many Allied pilots who, in spite of the high risk and the loss of several lives, brought us food and coal. It is incredible to try and starve a million-strong town as if it were a medieval castle.

I am still filled with gratitude to all these people – there was so much goodwill towards us even though we had caused immeasurable pain to so many others. I only wish that we did not belong to a nation which is again exporting weapons. It would be good if swords were turned into ploughshares everywhere.

My deepest appreciation is for my mother, who, surrounded by all the mayhem, never lost her nerve and protected and cared for us with much love.

Christine's Memories

Mine was perhaps too idyllic a beginning in East Prussia, in a village near Insterburg, Berschkallen (see map 4 for main places mentioned in text), which in 1936 was given the German name of Birken: a vicar, a teacher, a big vicarage with a large garden with special vegetable and fruit gardens. It was looked after by our grandfather from Breslau, who had just been released from concentration camp, having – because he was a social democrat - lost his position as senior Office of Works official of Breslau. Our capable grandmother took care of the housekeeping and instructed the maids. Then there was a little boy, eleven months later a girl (me, born 1938), chickens, ducks, geese, peacocks which all day long screeched and displayed their open tails and multicoloured pigs. We were close to the wood with its elks which 'listened into eternity', and with the howling of wolves during the long winter nights.

A little sister, born in the year 1942, enlivened this scene. I remember these first years as carefree, unthinkingly secure, active, full of ideas, when we happily hatched plots – not always appreciated by all – searching for the frog king in the deep well, letting the poor little pigs escape into the nearby field, pouring water for the bees to drink in their hive when it was very hot, starting to fell big trees with the toy saw from our Sunday wonder-bag, and so on ...light-heartedly 'fluttering like butterflies over meadows and fields'. Such was our fame.

As early as the year 1939, our father was called up to the war front as an observer and field vicar. From this moment on the entire parish work rested on my mother's shoulders even though she was not yet 30 years old. She felt it to be her responsibility to keep together the large and widely dispersed parish in these difficult (for the church) political times. People were seeking consolation and help from her, when her own heart was so heavy, as husbands, sons, fathers fell in the war. She also had to draw up 'Aryan certificates'. How many she attested in this way *(enabling them to prove to the authorities their Aryan, i.e. non-Jewish background and thus saving their lives)* we shall never know.

All these anxieties were kept from us children living in our idyllic world. This changed drastically when, alone on a wide empty field, I was surprised by an ear-shattering noise from a low-flying fighter plane. I had never seen a plane before. For the first time I **felt** that there was a sinister side to this war and that my father must be in great danger. (We did not know then that he had just survived Stalingrad.) I was shaken awake and, worried and upset, I started to notice the anxious faces of adults. Made restless and apprehensive, and trying to find help, I jumped from a high-flying swing and, looking at our house, I challenged God: 'Bring my father back from the war alive or else I shall never believe in you again!' I was four years old.

About this time I was staying with an uncle in Königsberg, whom I greeted on his return from his chancellery with 'Heil Hitler!' The usually kind uncle gave me a resounding smack on the ear. Later, after he refused to defend East Prussia's Gauleiter *(district commissioner)* Koch, he disappeared into a concentration camp for ever.

In early autumn 1943 my sister and I were sent to my Breslau grandparents, probably to lighten my mother's workload somewhat. Church services, christenings and funerals were conducted by my grandfather from Königsberg, but my mother carried out all the parish work in a more and more desolate community. To my great regret my brother had to stay back in Birken because he had to start school. Our first separation, a first earthquake.

Our grandparents had moved from Breslau into a rented apartment in Bad Obernigk. They looked after us with immense kindness. Going to the open-air swimming pools in summer, visiting the zoo and concerts in the park on Sundays – this was our small world. But still, a deep longing for my mother and brother tortured me, a loneliness which I could not share with anyone (decades later I read in my mother's diary from this time how greatly she suffered from the tearing apart of the family).

I can no longer remember how often we had to rush down into the air-raid shelters. I can only remember that is what we had to do and there is the memory of the darkness and the great silence. Every evening we had to pull down the blackout blinds 'to shut out the enemy'. How naive we were! A little later we had the idea of peeping through a tiny slit at the side of the blinds and saw the silver 'Christmas tree decorations' dropped from planes *(they were used to demarcate the next target for bombing)*, falling silently, eerily, lightening up the night. To this day I still do not like fireworks, however beautiful their shining displays may be.

Food became monotonous because we had no garden in Obernigk. Soup made with flour, potatoes, carrots and Sauerkraut, sometimes Quark *(a kind of cottage cheese)* was on our table and jam with turnips to make it go further for our breakfast rolls. But we did not yet suffer from hunger.

In August 1944 I started school three months before my sixth birthday. My school satchel was my grandfather's old briefcase which made me very unhappy when I saw the 'proper' satchels of my schoolmates. My favourite possessions in this large briefcase were the slate and my first reading book.

In late autumn of 1944 our mother and brother came from East Prussia to Obernigk. The atmosphere seemed to suggest that something terrible had happened. We heard that our aunt, my grandmother's youngest daughter, my mother's sister had died in childbirth, along with her baby boy, leaving behind little Hermann who was not yet one year old. He became part of our family as our little brother.

His home was in Sorau in Upper Lusatia where my mother now took my little sister Renate so that these two little ones could be looked after by a distant aunt. My mother, together with my grandfather, went back to East Prussia, where she had taken into the vicarage 19 women and children who had fled from the bombardment of Königsberg. The women had to be taken to a safe place first so that they could then continue their journey to the West. Our family was now scattered over East Prussia, Lusatia, Silesia; and our father, where was he?

In that freezing winter, when my mother and grandfather had to flee from East Prussia, mostly on foot through forests, we were told to evacuate Obernigk. This meant we had to appear next morning at the railway station to be transported on one of the horse-drawn carriages or sledges. On our arrival at the station we found that all the carriages and sledges were already over-full. This was our good luck. Later we heard that all the sledges had overturned and many people were badly hurt or lost their lives.

After we had spent an agonising day of uncertainty on the freezing railway station, a train arrived towards evening, and was stormed immediately by the crowd of waiting people. There were broken windows, frozen toilets, temperatures around minus 25 degrees centigrade. My grandmother wrapped my brother and me in Grandfather's wolf's fur, about the only thing she had managed to bring. Even my tortoise-doll and my little reading book had to stay behind. The train often stopped at night, completely blacked out, in the middle of fields to avoid detection by squadrons of enemy planes. We never knew when the journey would continue. Nevertheless, my grandmother held us out of the door when we needed the toilet. When we came back, Grandfather's wolf's fur had been stolen. The wagon was filled with the cries of desperate mothers whose children had frozen to death, or had died from illness.

After a lot of searching we managed to find the rest of our family in Sorau. Shortly after that the order to evacuate arrived here too. Our group of seven was supposed to go to Meissen *(near Dresden in Saxony)*, where our father had been able to find refuge for us with the families of two vicars. The platforms on the railway station of Sorau were so overcrowded with people and their luggage that it was difficult to find a space to put our feet. An incoming train tore apart one of the feather beds. In a dense cloud of feathers, which filled eyes, nose and mouth, the mass of people frantically fought to get onto the train. There were as many cries as feathers in the air as well as the desperate fear of getting left behind alone in this chaos and losing one's dearest.

Then our lives in Meissen started. On one of the many tracks outside the station there was a military transport train and

23

somehow our mother found the one in which our father stood – in a cattle truck behind blocked bars. A few words then the train started to move. I cried and waved my daddy goodbye, for the last time.

The house of vicar P, where we were given two permanently dark rooms, stood on the bank of the River Elbe, a few steps from the bridge over the Elbe. Every evening our grandparents walked a few minutes to their sleeping quarters with vicar S. This walk was along a stone wall, which was frequently under gunfire from the other side of the River Elbe. If we had to sleep where our grandparents were living, we had to walk along this stone wall all by ourselves. At some time this terrifying trip was stopped.

I made myself a little doll by pinching two of the carefully cut small pieces of toilet paper made of newspaper. This ended in severe reprimands.

Soon the air-raids became more frequent and were followed by a hurried rush into the air-raid shelter. Grandfather drummed into our heads that we must be able, in the dark, to grab immediately all the essential things, including those for the little ones who did not want to wake up. Once in the cellar we heard at first a distant growling, then nearer, the sound of the squadron of bombers fanning out, and then, while ducking our heads, the fly-over of the entire squadron and at last the disappearance of the squadron. Gone. Sirens sounded the All-Clear. This was repeated also on the night when thousands perished in Dresden and on the meadows by the River Elbe where thousands of refugees were camped. We scrambled out of our cellar into the courtyard and saw the sky above Dresden burning blood-red.

In the following days something unimaginable happened. Columns of horse-drawn carriages laden with something dark crossed the bridge over the River Elbe. It took a while before our children's eyes comprehended the incomprehensible. The load on the carriages was charred human bodies.

I did not then know Munch's painting 'The Cry' but now I would express the absolute horror of those days in that way.

My mother wanted to distract me and arranged for me to go to gymnastics. I arrived there late and saw lots of empty clothes hanging in the cloakroom. I fled in panic and never went back. Nor did I go any longer to swimming lessons; the wide indoor pool terrified me. The bridge over the Elbe was blown up (flying roof tiles buried the first tender green shoots of Grandfather's recently sown-out carrots), before armistice was declared on the 8th of May. For us this meant the end of our stay with the 'hospitable' vicars, where we had lived on soup and porridge made of water and corn, while their storage cellars were still packed to the brim.

My mother had managed to find a vegetable- and fruit-nursery. Mrs Friedel, whose husband had not yet returned, urgently needed help with the harvesting. On a hot May day, pushing a little pony cart and a doll's pram with big wheels laden with some crockery and utensils, for whose safety I was responsible, we walked the long distance from Meissen to Coswig. We were warmly welcomed with a table of food richly laden such as we had not seen for months. Aunt Friedel and my mother harvested, we helped, Grandmother ruled the roost in the kitchen and Grandfather gave lessons to us and the Friedels' children. We were in paradise. The only trouble was that the long period of severe hunger made itself felt: I had abscesses along my spine and legs. An endless daily torture of changing bandages started. Mrs Friedel's husband returned. The two women had formed a friendship which was to last their whole lives. However, the time of harvesting and with it of making ourselves useful was over.

Our grandmother from Königsberg, whose son-in-law was born in Halle on the River Saale, was able to find accommodation with a vicar in Halle. The latter had been asked to look after a large apartment belonging to a professor of theology who had fled to West Germany. Taking in our large family suited him just fine, as he was thus able to avoid the occupation of the whole apartment by Russians. However, two Russians were there already and they drummed on our bedroom door at night, shouting 'Woman, Woman!' This was terrible for our mother but also for us. Mother was sitting on the window sill, ready to jump. The ground was far below. These rogues were replaced by an educated *(Russian)* major, with whom we were allowed to listen to the children's radio station. We all had painful bites at night: bedbugs! Hunting for them in locked rooms was chaotic.

The hunger in Halle! Grandmother's dumplings, made with potato peelings and served with a sauce of flour and spiced with marjoram, were a feast. At one time, when our larder was completely empty, I found a bag with white powder on a wall. Grandmother tested it first to check that it was edible. After that we went to sleep with stomachs filled with lovely flour soup. Once, at the beginning of a month when I had the entire ration cards for the month stolen, all 30 girls in my class gave me their school dinner bread rolls. What incredible solidarity! Some of them needed their rolls themselves. That month we lived on four dry rolls a day.

Grandfather was sent to hospital with suspected cancer, but his terrible pain was caused by parts of his intestines rubbing against each other. I was sent into the country. A bus dropped me and the other children at the inn in the village of Kossebau, near Stendahl. All the other children immediately found their host families. I alone remained from that midday until the evening when a farmer took pity on me. The first thing he did was put me on the scales: at nearly nine years old I weighed barely 18 kilos.

Farmer B was our great good fortune. He let my mother come as well and we were allowed to glean his fields. A year before that, we had had to fight for every single ear of corn and spend the nights on three chairs in an inn. Now we sat at the kitchen table removing the ears one by one from each corn, then grinding the valuable grains in a coffee grinder. I remember blisters on the palms of my hands.

Grandfather was given an allotment in Halle. It was a former runway; Grandfather, my brother and I had to dig up and cart away each individual paving stone, to get at the earth beneath. Grandfather then turned it into a wonder garden with potatoes, vegetables and tobacco. Grandmother squeezed syrup from sugar beet (wherever did she collect it?) by using the weight of us children on top of a press. At Christmas we made a large gingerbread house using *our flour* and *our sugar syrup*! To our dismay Mother invited about 'a hundred' children to the feast beneath our decorations of newspaper bunting, because 'other children are worse off than us', she told us.

At this time we put on many plays and acted in them, using our own scripts and our own stage settings. Co-actors were the neighbours' and Russian children. In Mother's diary there is this entry: 'The children have become old for their age, are precocious and only play at war.'

In about March 1949 our time in Halle came to a sudden end: a Russian lady had warned my mother that the Communist Party had designs on my brother in terms of moving him to Moscow. Mother took both boys and fled via Berlin, hoping to take one of the airlift planes *(to West Germany)*. However, she did not have enough money for the flight. 'Why are you crying?' a stranger asked her in the overcrowded Berlin airport and told her to wait for him. He brought tickets, which he had been selling to others for double the price. Such unexpected empathy existed then.

Grandfather and one of my mother's friends took my sister and me to a village near the border *(between East and West Germany)* so that we could cross the 'green border' to West Germany. We were caught, put into prison and then sent back. Grandfather, who did not really want to go to the West, decided after several such failed trips that, with my grandmother, the four of us should flee together to the West. In a dark pub a woman was waiting for us at night; she was supposed to lead us through a brown coal field which was full of landmines. Without making a sound! The only way I could get my sister to be silent was by telling her that we would all die if she continued to cry (but I myself was crying inside because my grandparents were far ahead). The rest is a blackout. When I woke up I found myself in a white bed, someone pulling back white curtains, letting in the sun and crying, 'Good God, the poor kids.'

A renewed disruption of the family started in the spring of 1949. The grandparents were staying with their son in

Hamburg. Little Hermann, whose father suddenly remembered him, was in an orphanage in Bielefeld, where the 'good sisters' took away his last remaining toy, his little bear. The little boy was completely lost. Our mother with my brother was in a tiny room in an attic in Wuppertal, staying with a First World War widow. It later turned out that her son had had to bury our father near Stalingrad. My sister Renate and I found ourselves in an orphanage in Schwelm. We were given one bed for the two of us and a heavy military blanket in the middle of a large hall with 25 girls.

On Sundays our mother visited us, followed always by goodbyes till the next Sunday. How long did this go on? As with so many things, I have never asked. The change came when my father's brother, a paediatrician, took us to his home in Mettmann, near Wuppertal. This felt like family: Dad, Mum and children. My uncle let me take the entry examination for the gymnasium; every morning I went to school, singing with joy. The joy was short lived. We had to go back to the orphanage. There, as someone attending the gymnasium, I was treated like a leper; at the gymnasium they also treated me, coming from the orphanage, like a leper. I could not keep down the watery morning porridge and I went to school without breakfast. I had to sit in the back row; apparently I cried a lot, had the wrong schoolbooks and was thought to be stupid. It was unreasonable to expect my mother to buy me new schoolbooks. The mother of a classmate, Barbara, suggested that her daughter should bring me to their home. I had feelings of infinite happiness, away from the atmosphere in the orphanage - mother, father, children. This was the beginning of a life-long friendship, sisterhood even.

Thanks – seen from hindsight – to my undiagnosed illness with a high temperature, the orphanage paediatrician found a small flat for us. Two rooms, a kitchen and a toilet half-way down the stairs to be shared with another family. There were no windows. When a mighty thunderstorm passed over the house we were terrified. The attic above us had no roof; it was completely open to the skies.

Our furniture consisted of a small iron stove where we could cook our only food, unripe pears, one bed for the four of us with a deep hole in the middle of the mattress, which we filled with clothing not currently worn. Every night my mother read us stories. In spite of everything, we felt very happy.

But it was not the whole story. Our grandparents were very unhappy in Hamburg and moved in with us in our minute flat, but they were very helpful. We got by on out-working (*Heimarbeit*): hour after hour we laboured, including us children, our contribution to our survival. We never complained, even when the other children were playing outside. Once the vicar visited us and thought it very nice to see the whole family happily working around the table at home. My sister shouted at him: 'Out-working is terrible work.' The vicar never came back. God's man was never interested that my brother and I had to share a pair of shoes; luckily one had to be at school in the morning, the other in the afternoon. The most important thing was to be punctual for the changeover of shoes.

During the summer of 1950, we children were sent for three months to distant relatives in Switzerland. It was paradise and Utopia in one. We were allowed to be children again. There were no ruins or collapsed buildings. The relatives were kind to us, cheerful and uncomplicated. I got my first pair of shoes in years that fitted me (Bally shoes), our aunt brought book after book for us to read, a bowl of fruit was replenished every morning, there was meat at lunchtime and on Saturdays a big bath was filled in the laundry room with water just for you. I inherited the beautiful dresses of my same-age 'big sister'. From then on, I was no longer ridiculed at school about wearing the same poor clothes.

A little after that Adenauer managed to get prisoners-of-war released from Russia. The names were read out on the radio. Listening to it, we felt drained of life and hope when the letter S (the initial letter of our family name) passed by.

My grandfather fought a long time to receive his pension, which he had lost in Nazi Germany. He obtained compensation only after promising to sign a document saying that he would never release the names of people who put him into the concentration camp, nor of those who maltreated him there. Only from 1952 onwards did a sort of 'normal' life start for us in a more spacious flat with a bath. My mother got a position as a part-time teacher in a school in Schwelm. Even there the director prevented her from receiving the pension due to her.

In spite of all the disastrous things we experienced, as well as those not even mentioned here, I feel grateful that we came through these difficult times relatively unscathed. I am sure that I speak for my courageous, strong mother as well.

Dörthe's Memories

I was born on a Sunday, the 27th August 1939, the fourth child of my parents in Meuselwitz, near Altenburg in Thuringia (see map 5 for main places mentioned in text). Not only was I a Sunday child I was also a peacetime child – but only just.

On the first of September 1939, German troops marched into Poland and thus started WWII. My mother always told us that, a week before that event, rationing cards had been handed out to the population so that people were prepared for the coming action. I ask myself how worried my mother was to be bringing her fourth child into the world at this time. For propaganda purposes we were told that it was Poland's attack on Germany and 'from this morning at 4.45a.m., fire is being returned' – today we know better. My mother was still confined to bed after my birth; I was born at home, as was common at this time, and a local midwife called every day. What might these two women have talked about?

My eldest brother was born in 1933, my sister in 1935 and my second brother in 1937. At the beginning of 1939 my family had moved to Meuselwitz and was thus new there. Was my mother feeling lonely? My father was called up in 1940 as a soldier and at this time my mother was pregnant with her fifth child. My third brother was born in November 1940. How did she feel then? And how did she manage everything with these small children?

My father was 'lucky'. He was fighting with the army in Norway and was perhaps spared the worst brutalities of war. But we really don't know anything about this because, like many fathers, he did not talk about it after the war. My youngest brother and I only knew my father from his short home leaves and did not recognise him when he returned after the war from a prisoner-of-war camp.

Our mother had to get us five children through the war by herself. At first, the war seemed to be happening at a distance from us. However, families evacuated from the heavily bombarded Ruhr and Saar territories arrived and we squeezed into fewer rooms in order to be able to accommodate two families in one house. We shared one garden with our neighbours and there were always a lot of children and adults, which was great for us. Memories from my childhood include only a small area around the house and the garden up to the garden gate. I didn't dare to go any further; my brothers and sisters were more adventurous than me. They said that I was an anxious child, but perhaps I got this with my mother's milk?

Our town was spared bombardments until November 1944, and then the first devastating bombardment took place. Nevertheless, even before that time sirens howled whenever a formation of bomber planes flew over us in the direction of Leipzig. Whenever the sirens went, mostly at night, we had to go to the cellar of the neighbouring house because our cellar consisted of only one small room. Every time, fear and agitation made my older sister need to go on the potty, trying my mother's patience greatly. Even today, howling sirens remind me of these bombardments.

The last, heavy Anglo-American bombardment was on the 20th February 1945 when 80% of our town was destroyed. This bombardment resulted in many dead (the youngest victim was four weeks old), badly wounded and homeless people. The bombs were supposed to hit the nearby factory which was manufacturing extensive amounts of ammunition and other armaments, for instance anti-tank hand guns. The factory was 80% demolished, but sadly many bombs were dropped too early and completely destroyed many houses in the town and the neighbouring large estate. After the All-Clear signal we saw that everything was burning fiercely and that many birds had died in the fire. Our house had lost its roof and doors and the windows had been blown out. The sight of it was a terrible shock for me and some days the trauma still haunts me. When my mother saw how deeply affected I was she tried to console me and said that we were very lucky to have survived unhurt. Yes, we survived this heavy bombardment in contrast to many, many others. Our family had spent this terrible night in two different cellars. My eldest brother had contracted scarlet fever and was running a very high temperature, so that my mother had spent the night with him in the little cellar of our own house. The rest of us were in the cellar of the neighbouring house. One can imagine how happy we were when we all came back together unhurt. My brother was taken on the same day in one of the first transports to the hospital in the neighbouring big town, where he stayed for six weeks.

Around our house lay a lot of rubble. I remember that my younger brother and I helped to carry the rubble to the road in little buckets. All of the factories had stopped working, gas and water pipes were destroyed. Many men had died in the war or were prisoners-of-war. The town had to accommodate many evacuees and re-settlers and was responsible for the starving prisoners-of-war and forced labourers in the camps. The destroyed ammunition factory had been using many foreign workers from all over Europe and also prisoners from the concentration camps at Buchenwald and Auschwitz. Many inhabitants of the town did not at that time know about this. I only remember that people talked about foreign workers. Many only found out afterwards about the whole extent of the cruelties of that war.

After this bombardment life was chaotic: food was very scarce and it was difficult for our mother to feed us five children and herself. We exchanged silver cutlery, clothes and other objects of value with the farmers for bread, potatoes and flour. Many farmers exploited this situation and I often saw my mother looking very sad. The liberation of our little town by American troops in 1945 brought with it the end of the war and twelve years of Nazi control. Children sought contact with the American soldiers, as did my twelve-year-old brother, who had learnt a little English at school and could make himself understood. He exchanged stamps with an American soldier, who soon started to bring his laundry to my mother to be washed and ironed. In this way we obtained soap and some food, which made us more than happy. However, the Americans soon had to leave and with them, sadly, our friendly American soldier. My brother kept in contact with him and his family for a long time, and they sent us regular Care parcels in the 1950s. These were a very welcome support.

Following the Treaty of Yalta an exchange of territory took place; the Americans left and the Soviet army marched in and occupied our town. I often went shopping for my mother and once I was surprised on the way home by the endless number of tanks which thundered along the main street. Together with other people I stood at the side of the road and watched the Russian troops marching in. Suddenly my mother stood beside me – she had been very worried about my lengthy absence. Although I was only six years old, even I realised that the adults watched the entry of the Russians with great anxiety.

After the joy of the liberation by the American troops, many wondered anxiously what would happen now. After all, the Nazis' propaganda had painted a terrible picture of the Russians (and, as one heard later, the town's population suffered particularly badly from plundering and rape by the first Soviet troops marching into the town).

Now the terrible post-war period started with its hunger and the clearing away of ruins and debris. We often went gleaning with our mother, walking over the fields after the farmer had harvested and allowed the general population onto his fields. I remember the occasion when my eldest brother boiled all the potatoes which he had collected and brought home, and ate them all by himself. The boys were always very hungry.

My father finally returned from a camp for prisoners-of-war in France in 1947. He let himself be released first to his mother and two sisters in the British zone to get fed and only then came to his family in the Russian-occupied zone. I am sure that was difficult for him as he guessed what awaited him. At first he saw no way to get his family over into the West. My father was a stranger to my younger brother and me, and my brother asked my mother "When is the stranger leaving?" We too were strangers to my father and he experienced the same fate as many soldiers returning from the war. How were they expected to find and to fill their place in their families again? Their children did not know them, the eldest sons had often taken the place of the absent fathers and did not accept their authority any longer, and even the women had become more independent and did not return to their previous roles. We were never again able to establish a close relationship with our father, and perhaps that is why he was so very happy about the birth of my little sister in 1953, since there he saw a new opportunity. For our mother, who was nearly 44, it was not such a happy occasion and I, at 13 years old, worried about where to get a pram.

A new job meant that the family had to move in 1948 to a neighbouring town. The seventh October 1949, saw the foundation of the German Democratic Republic, the GDR. My father had thought about fleeing for some time, and in October 1950 we started to plan in earnest. My elder sister was sent temporarily to relatives in Saxony; from there she travelled later on to Berlin. We travelled to East-Berlin, taking only the minimum of luggage, and from there we took the 'Schnellbahn' *(a kind of above-ground tube)* to West Berlin. There we stayed with a family we knew in Berlin-Zehlendorf. This was very difficult for my mother, as she had to leave behind all our possessions. She particularly regretted having spent so much time bottling 400 jars of fruit, which also had to be left behind in the house.

A few things such as bedding, dresses and the sewing machine came with friends to Kleinmachnow, near Berlin, from where we could collect them bit by bit. We were officially recognised as political refugees. Soon we got a small flat in an attic, where the seven of us and a boarder, whom we had to feed as well, lived together, until my little sister was born, when there was not enough space for a boarder.

My father was not able to get a foothold professionally and fell very ill in 1954/55 with cancer. He died in 1956, aged 53. Now our mother was alone again with four children; my eldest brother had meanwhile emigrated to Canada and my eldest sister was training as a nurse with the Red Cross in Seesen in the Harz mountains. This left my two brothers, my little sister and me with my mother. We could finally move into a flat provided by the town; our own flat, without strangers, even if it was still very small and cramped. My mother lived to her 91st year and lived an uncomplaining, unassuming life. Her calmness and her quiet courage have always been a great example to us. She died in 2000.

What emotions do I have about my childhood in the war, the post-war years, the hunger, the flight and the difficult beginnings in Berlin, which was for a long time a field of ruins? I, like many others, probably repressed many thoughts and feelings. Of course, it was a good childhood too, in a small town, with a beautiful garden, with brothers and sisters, within the safety of a family, even though my father was missing for the first seven years. This was perhaps the reason why I had such a close relationship with my mother.

But there was also a lot of fear – even in the early days when the war seemed far away. There was fear for our absent father and the adults' fear which they tried to hide from us children, and which was probably transferred to me in the womb. Today we know how easily this can happen. Also, the ridiculous idea that children don't understand a lot of what is going on has been found to be a false comfort. We did not talk about the fear, not at all with our parents and not even with our sisters and brothers. My brothers did not know what fear was: "That's how it was then," they said.

Only now do I think differently about it all. Even my husband, who was born in 1938 in East Prussia and who fled with his mother and sister in January/February1945, over the frozen (*Baltic*) Haff to relatives in Berlin, does not 'remember' anything. His family also does not talk about their experiences. My husband's father had been a prisoner-of-war after fighting at the Eastern Front; when he returned to the family, he too was a stranger to them. After his parents divorced my husband had little opportunity to get to know his father, let alone to ask him about the war.

One of my sisters-in-law was born in 1936 in Pommerania, the third of five children. Her father fell in the war, her grandfather, mother and the five children fled shortly before the end of the war from Pommerania to relatives in Berlin. Her mother died during the flight, her little baby brother six months later. A great-aunt brought up the four children. Here too, no one spoke about their wartime experiences.

And if we had asked? Would we have got an answer? And would we have liked to hear it? Today we know that it is very important to talk to each other, because the traumas experienced during the war by a whole generation of children silently get carried over into the next generation. Our parents did not know any better and neither did we. We were dealing with survival, with rebuilding, with forgetting – with a whole range of guilt and shame, not only of the individual but also of the whole nation. So it is a good thing that we are now starting to talk.

Erika's Memories

There was still peace – but there were already signs of the coming conflict in many places when I was born in February 1939, in the Steglitz district of Berlin (see map 6 for main places mentioned in text). War started on the first of September 1939, and in the same month I was admitted to the Charity Hospital with polio – a great shock for my parents. Many of the younger medics had already been called up to the front and, according to my parents, there was considerable chaos.

We spent the first months of the war in Berlin – experiencing the first air raid on the town there. When an air raid alarm sounded – mostly at night – everything had to happen very quickly: I was fetched from my cot, my small 'survival case' was put into my hands and down we went into the air raid cellar in the house, where all the residents of the house were gathered. I can clearly remember that the cellar in this old house was very crooked and twisted and that we doubted whether anyone would find us should we be hit by a bomb.

At the end of 1942 we were evacuated to Cotbus, to my grandparents' on my father's side. Since at that time my mother's mother lived with us, my grandparents had to find space for three extra people. My father was at this time working in the central administration of the German Railway in Berlin's Mitte district. His job had been classified as 'indispensable', and therefore he did not have to go to war but had to man his post in Berlin. Nevertheless, at the beginning of 1945 he was called up to the 'Volkssturm'. This 'home front army' consisted mainly of old men.

The flat in Cotbus was very overcrowded and there were difficulties in the daily routine of living together. My mother was pregnant and in April 1943 my little sister came into this world in the most difficult of circumstances. After another heavy air raid on Cotbus we moved to Calbe on the Saale, to the house of my father's brother. My uncle was at the front and the entire family (grandmothers, grandfathers, etc.) was now assembled there. My mother, grandmother and we two children were billeted in the storeroom of the former grocer's shop – between barrels of gherkins and herring– and, of course, the room was not heated and accordingly very cold. We were not exactly welcome and it was only much later that I found out the reasons for this rejection.

We lived there in quite poor circumstances until the end of the war. At first the Americans arrived, then the Russians. The street barriers which had been constructed were simply overrun by the tanks – a big event for us children. A strict curfew was enforced. If someone did not obey the curfew, he or she was taken away by the Russians and incarcerated. Several people disappeared and were never seen again.

After the capitulation on the 8th of May, 1945, all refugees were told to return to their original place of residence – regardless of whether they still had a place to live there or not. My father came from Berlin to collect us. We reached our apartment in Berlin-Steglitz under perilous circumstance. The house was still standing and our flat was just about habitable in spite of the damage done by bombardments, so we settled in as well as we could. There was neither food nor fuel available to buy. The black market was flourishing: any remaining possessions were bartered for food. My mother and grandmother went in overcrowded trains on foraging trips into the surrounding countryside. But of course, several thousand people from Berlin did the same and soon there was nothing left to forage.

My parents had an allotment in Blankenfelde, south of Berlin. As soon as the S-bahn (*Schnellbahn* = *overland tube*) was running again, my grandmother could work in the garden again and our food supply was somewhat improved. Meanwhile on our balcony in Berlin Steglitz we grew tomatoes, and later there were rabbits – grandmother had organised them from somewhere. Life consisted mainly of 'organising'.

The ruins of the houses around us were part of our everyday existence, as were the graves of people hastily buried in the front gardens, the crosses surmounted by a steel helmet on the graves of soldiers who had fallen in the last battle for Berlin – a terrible memory for me.

I started school in the autumn – with two weeks' delay, because no one had realised in the permanent chaos that school had started. At the same time treatment for my leg, which was partially paralysed from polio, began again at the Oskar-Helene Hospital.

We children loved to play in the surrounding ruins, especially in the ruins of half-bombed-out villas in the Dahlem district of Berlin, in spite of having been strictly forbidden to do so. I got a few serious injuries on my right hand but nothing else.

My father was allowed to stay on in his old job. He had managed not to join the NSDAP (*National Sozialistische Deutsche Arbeiter Partei* = *National Socialist German Workers' Party*) in spite of his status as a civil servant. We were very grateful that we still had our father and provider. Berlin became a city divided into four zones and Steglitz belonged to the American zone. But since my father's work was in East Berlin (the Russian zone), he was paid in East German money. He could exchange only a very small part of his income at the favourable rate of 1:1 into West German money, so I travelled every other day on the S-bahn to the Friedrichstrasse *(the border to the Russian zone)* to buy bread and other things using East German money. Often there was nothing to buy and I had to return home without having bought anything.

The constant hunger left its mark. My mother contracted tuberculosis and was very ill for many months. Every second day I was sent to the hospital at the Heidelberg Square with a warm meal which my grandmother had cooked. But because I was not allowed to see my mother (because she was in quarantine) I had to hand over the pot and its contents at the gate. We very much hoped that she actually received the meal but never knew the truth. During this time, we took in a young girl from Silesia who had lost her parents and her homeland.

Then the next disaster happened – the-Soviets closed the border, so that all supply routes to West Berlin were cut off *(the Berlin Blockade)*. The Allies organised an air-lift; every two minutes the 'raisin bombers' touched down, American and British planes flew into Tempelhof airport, later the French flew into Gatow and Tegel airports. Two and a half million inhabitants of West Berlin were supplied with sufficient food stuff – all in tins. Even coal was flown in to keep the power stations of West Berlin just about going. Nevertheless, there were frequent power cuts. The Russian closure of the borders lasted from 24 June 1948 to 12 May 1949, nearly a whole year! My little sister also contracted tuberculosis and was flown in one of the returning coal-planes to Stuttgart to our uncle. She stayed there an entire year. That was a terrible time for me with my mother in hospital and my little sister far away. Then one day, my father did not return home from his work in East Berlin. Nobody knew what had happened. After three days of uncertainty he arrived home. The Russians had moved the entire Department to Karlshorst, an eastern part of Berlin, into the Russian headquarters. Nobody knew why.

After the end of the air-lift we were allowed back into our allotment and life became a bit more normal. Father kept bees; there was even honey to eat!

Around this time, when I was in secondary school, we went on a school trip to the 'Funkturm' (*a tall wireless tower*). I was given the money for the tube journey, carefully counted out at home. However, I desperately wanted to get to the top of the 'Funkturm' so I took the money which was meant for the return journey and used it to buy a entry ticket to the Funkturm. Travelling home was very comfortable – in a French army jeep, which I had simply stopped. I knew a bit of French already and the kind soldiers took me all the way home to Steglitz right up to the front door. Up on the balcony stood my mother, watching as her daughter got out of a military vehicle and I could guess what would follow - a huge box on the ear that really hurt! I never hitchhiked again.

In May 1952 we had to give up our allotment. It was situated 2 km from Lichtenrade, the border between East and West Berlin, in the so-called 'Zone' (the Russian-occupied zone), and people from West Berlin were no longer allowed to go there. It was not till March 1990, with the reunification of East and West Germany, that I saw our allotment again.

The East-West situation became more and more precarious – our family was put under pressure to move to East Berlin. One day my father found that his desk had been thoroughly searched and he decided not to return to his post in East Berlin; it had become too dangerous. After a short period of unemployment he found work at the central office of the State Railway in Minden in Westphalia in West Germany. We left Berlin and our beautiful apartment in the summer of 1953 and moved to Minden. I had to leave my beloved school and all my friends – at the age of 14 this was a hard experience. My sister and I were put on the train to Helmstedt, West Germany, where my father was awaiting us. The journey from Berlin to Helmstedt lasted nine hours, through the 'Zone', often interrupted by controls carried out by the East German 'People's Police'. Meanwhile, my mother travelled with our furniture lorry – there too everything was checked thoroughly – right down to the last spoon.

My memories of the time in Minden are not very positive: the new school was particularly horrid. As a so-called refugee child I was bullied. The taunt was always: 'Why don't you go back to where you came from?' Our history lessons took us only up to 1918! Not even the 'golden' years of the 1920s, the Weimar Republic, were mentioned, let alone the '1000-year German Reich'. I left this school after my 'Mittlere Reife' (*O-levels*). I filled the time until I was 17 and could then start the training to become a technical assistant in chemical and biological laboratories by attending a business school to learn shorthand and typing. The summer term of 1956 saw my return to Berlin, where I lived in a rented room in our former house in Berlin-Steglitz.

Since my father spent the entire war years in Berlin, working for the German Railway, he was very well informed about what happened on the front. In contrast to most fathers and to my mother, he was always ready to talk with me about the war and post-war years.

Helga's Memories

On the ninth of March 1945 we had to leave our home in Lauenburg in Pomerania (see map 7 for main places mentioned in text) for good. A few weeks earlier we had stood by the road; we were supposed to have been taken by soldiers to Danzig so that we could leave the country on board the *Gustloff*. But after several hours when we were frozen through and through and no military vehicle had come, we went home again. That was a lucky day for us. The *Gustloff* sank with all lives lost.

This time we were taken along in a hospital train full of the wounded. The soldiers had nothing to eat and asked my mother and her friend to fetch some preserved food and wine from their cellars. They said that the train would remain for a while at the station. My aunt, one of my mother's sisters, stayed with us children. I was nine years old, my sisters ten and six.

After a while the train was shunted to a siding at the freight station. We were frightened that our mothers would not be able to find us and kept getting out of the train, shouting for them. All stations were without light then, because of the air-raids.

In the distance we could hear the approaching Russian front and the sky over Danzig was red with raging fires. After we had spent several very anxious hours our mothers returned with the provisions for the soldiers. Nobody at the station had been able to tell them where our train had got to. Two days later the Russian troops arrived in Lauenburg.

When we arrived in Danzig, we were first taken to a spacious children's home in Danzig-Neufahrwasser. A night bombardment terrified us: it whistled and droned, windowpanes exploded and we children crawled underneath the tables in the day room. We had experienced air-raids in Lauenburg in our air-raid shelters, but the bomber planes had flown over our town bound for Danzig. This was altogether different. In the morning after the raid we were transferred to the shipyard in Gotenhafen 'Gdingen'. There we lay on straw and waited for the ship.

At last it happened! We were to be taken on the *Mars* to Denmark, which was occupied by the Germans. However, mine-sweepers had to clear the way first as the Baltic was mined, so the journey lasted several days. Provisions were getting scarce. Ship's biscuits, thick round ones, were handed out. We were happy but my sister Eva discovered that they were full of maggots. Nevertheless, we tried to eat around them. The toilets were getting more and more busy; every family had someone standing in the queue so that other members could get there faster when stomach pain started. Many were ill. We knew that the *Gustloff* had been sunk and the fear that we too would drown was strong.

In Copenhagen we were at first accommodated in schools, several families to one classroom. Our beds were sacks of straw. At regular intervals there was delousing. I can't remember everything but our mothers and other women organised varied evening entertainments with lectures, songs and piano playing in the school's assembly hall. I remember even a tight-rope walker in the school yard.

Many children got dysentery; the sanitary facilities were appalling and this intestinal illness spread fast. I too became ill and lost consciousness for several days. I shall never forget the image of a mother, who did not want to give up her dead two-year-old child she carried in her arms, and who ran screaming through the corridors.

On the 8th of May, the day of the Nazi capitulation, we suddenly heard shooting in the schoolyard. Danish Nazis shot at Danish freedom fighters; one man was shot dead. We were not allowed near the windows and had to sit indoors until everything was over.

We now hoped to be able to get home soon, but Germany was destroyed. There was nowhere for us to live and there was no food. Denmark fed the German refugees, who were supposed to have been about 250,000, from 1945 to 1949.

We could no longer stay in the schools in Copenhagen. The German soldiers had left the occupied countries and their barracks were now used to house refugees. We were shipped from Copenhagen to Aalberg in Jutland, which was a former airport. The barracks in which we were accommodated were full of bugs. Every now and then they were sprayed with chemicals and we had to move our bunk beds outside. As covers we were given blankets made of brown crepe paper stuffed with wood pulp (*cellulose*), making a kind of quilt. At night we could hear the bugs dropping onto our paper quilts and were afraid of their bites, which left nasty, itchy bumps.

Our camp was quite large. We had lessons, classes with several age-groups together. The journey to school was difficult; there were many sandstorms and in winter there were snowstorms. The teacher was a small man, one of the few men amongst the refugees, who were either unfit or too old for recruitment into the army. He taught us a lot.

Three to four families were living in each room of the barracks. We separated off each family's space by putting up ropes over which we threw army blankets. We burnt peat in a small stove to heat our rooms. The stove pipe went out through the window. We each got our ration of peat and because we were often cold our mothers once stole some peat, which was stored in a large hall. Of course, they were caught and had to go for a few hours to the camp prison. We were very embarrassed.

Around our camp there was barbed wire. We were guarded by Danes who sat in open guard towers. Two of the guards were very friendly and often brought us sweets. One once gave me a red, checked handkerchief because I had a runny nose; I kept it many decades. We children had hardly any personal belongings. All our toys and dolls had been left behind at home. We left, carrying rucksacks, which our mothers had sewn from linen towels, containing essentials only.

During the two and a half years of refugee camp we grew out of our shoes and clothes. Some of the old men in our camp carved wooden clogs for us. Dresses were sewn by hand using the army stores' checked bed linen. Some girls, including me, spun thread from cotton wool with simple spindles. From this yarn and some threads pulled from red-brown furniture covers, we knitted jumpers and we made ripple-cloth jumpers from *(first aid)* bandages which we cut into strips. Of course, these were as stiff as boards.

The women in the camp were often in despair because they had heard nothing from relatives in Germany and nothing from their husbands: were they in prison, were they still alive? Some received news and were happy; others had their fortunes told to grasp a little hope.

If you provided proof that you had a flat in Germany you could leave Denmark in one of the transportations. War widows and their children were sent to West Germany. My mother did not know that my father had already fallen in April 1945. However, she wanted to get back to Germany to see if she could find out something. A friend managed to get her a permit of residence to move to Sonneberg in Thuringia in East Germany. My aunt, my father's sister, had not dared to tell my mother of my father's death for fear that she might take her own life, as many women in the camp had done.

In August 1947 we were transported to Germany, first by ship, then by rail. The Danish government had sent along a carriage full of grain for Germany, which was behind the engine and immediately behind that was our luggage. Suddenly, near Stralsund, a fire broke out. The carriages behind the engine were burning fiercely. We all ran out of the train. Now the only things we had left were what we were wearing. It was said that the fire was caused by sparks from the engine, but there were also rumours of sabotage.

We were lodged in holiday houses in Eggesin, in Mecklenburg, in the Russian zone. We had to stay there some time in quarantine. Russian soldiers belonging to the occupying army were also living nearby. A few of the young girls had flirted with the Russians during the day. At night the drunken Russians returned and because they could not get at the girls they smashed up doors and windows and shouted loudly. We had barricaded ourselves in the rooms and once again were shivering with fright.

The singed luggage from the train was laid out in the town square. Passengers came forward to collect their belongings, but sometimes more than one family laid claim to the same piece of luggage, and there were quarrels and very unpleasant scenes. For a long time our clothes smelled of the fire they had survived.

After the quarantine we all travelled to the places for which we had obtained a permit of residence. My mother, my two sisters and I were given a room with a butcher and innkeeper in Sonneberg in Thuringia. In this one room we lived, slept, cooked and did our homework.

The year 1947 was a year of hunger in the former East Zone, particularly for people without a garden and without possessions which they could have bartered. My mother found work in a clothing factory. Eva and I went into the countryside to scavenge. We were happy if we could bring home three potatoes and a few slices of bread. We always had stomach ache and at night dreamt of huge cakes which, however, tasted of nothing. After harvesting time we went gleaning in the fields.

After the train journey from Denmark, my youngest sister, Renate, had to go into hospital with a perforated appendix. She was eight years old, and my mother had to push her in a buggy a long way to the hospital. No ambulance was available. When we visited her she always had a slice of bread with paté, which she did not like, in the drawer of her bedside table. Below it was the chamber pot.

By and by we discovered the whereabouts of relatives and friends through the Red Cross, amongst them an elderly couple from our home town, whose son had fallen in the war. Because at this time, at thirteen years old, I weighed only 24 kg, I was invited to spend the school holidays with them to recuperate.

My mother paid some 'Schleuser'(*people who helped others to cross the border illegally*) to take me under cover of darkness across the border into West Germany. At the station in Neustadt I was caught by the railway police, while changing my wet socks for a dry pair. As I was crying bitterly, they showed mercy and took me in their official car to Höxter on the River Weser. There I saw American soldiers, who sat eating deep-fried pancakes (*'Berliner'*) and peanuts. I must have stared at them because, as they were leaving, they threw the bags with the remains into my lap.

Next day, with the change of diet, I got a huge 'water belly' and my aunt, as I called her, took me to the doctor. To start with, I was given a diet of thin porridge, which I like to eat even today! The couple in Höxter offered to let me stay with them and finish my schooling there.

For a long time I could not see my mother and my sisters, because the border between East and West Germany got more and more difficult to cross, and Sonneberg was declared a 'prohibited area'. We were very happy when travelling became easier and when, in 1989, the Wall came down. The many years of separation had not been easy for either side.

Henriette's Memories

I was born in Perleberg (see map 8) on the first of November 1937, the second child in my family. My brother was two years older than me. In 1947 another little girl was born. Perleberg is a county town in the northwest of Brandenburg, which has been a military garrison town for a long time. We lived in a house built for two families which we had inherited from my paternal grandparents. The house, together with another block of flats and my father's workshops, was on a large piece of land. My father, like his father before him, was a professional painter and decorator.

In the very first year of the war, the business had to be closed down, and the apprentices and skilled workers were drafted into the war. My father was called up as a soldier at the airport control in Perleberg. The airport, formerly for gliders, was just outside the town. At some point my father was sent to Pinneberg, near Hamburg, where he was trained as a radio operator. He was then sent to the East, but not directly to the front. He had to produce drawings interpreting the movements of air traffic around the field of conflict.

Perleberg itself was hit by only one bomb, probably by accident, but there were countless air- raids on the airport. Many bomber formations flew over, always in the direction of Berlin. That is why in the last years of the war we lived with constant air-raid alarms. We often had to go into a cellar at school. The cellar in our house served as the air-raid shelter for all of the tenants of the neighbouring block of flats, as well as for ourselves. At the door of the cellar it said in large letters 'Suitable as air-raid shelter for 15 people'. How reassuring! At night it was terrible to have to go into the shelter; my brother often refused to go in.

There still seemed to have been enough food. My mother's parents had a very small grocer's shop in their ground-floor flat, separated from their living room. My grandfather was a WWI invalid, and had supplemented his small pension in this way. They sold butter, cheese and quark (*cottage cheese*), of course, in exchange for ration tokens. Every Friday, when the dairyman from the country delivered his goods, our grandmother gave us children quark, mixed with jam or sugar. 'Quark makes you strong, but quark alone gives you bow legs,' she would say, smiling. We also had a garden with an orchard and we grew vegetables; how valuable all this food was in these bad times!

About 1942, one of the families in the block of flats in our backyard was joined by their daughter from Berlin with her three sons, all about our age. They had been evacuated. My grandparents in their house at the front of the yard were joined by my aunt and her two-year- old daughter from Berlin-Lankwitz. They too had fled the bombardments. There were now quite a number of children playing on our land, well looked after by their mothers. We did not feel their anxieties and their worries. All our fathers were in the war.

At the beginning of the winter of 1944/45 the treks of refugees from Eastern Prussia reached Perleberg. They passed along our road in an uninterrupted stream with their horse-drawn wagons, packed to the tops, heading west to the bridge over the river Elbe near Wittenberg. Some stopped at our place and our mothers would help them as best they could. These treks made a very strong impression on me: I saw that you could use carpets to make a roof. Furthermore, I learnt that it was tremendously important to have many blankets when fleeing. Even today I appreciate woollen blankets on all excursions!

Now we began to have some experience of the war. A house belonging to the Protestant community in our neighbourhood was requisitioned as an army hospital. We children, curious and without fear, watched full of sympathy as the wounded were carried into the large hall. They were probably only slightly wounded soldiers and they were not stationed there for long. Nevertheless, their appearance shocked us greatly.

From March 1945 it became difficult to hold lessons at school: the rooms were needed for new refugees. Air-raids were becoming still more frequent. Tank barriers were built on the roads, and they frightened us, making us believe that the tanks would just roll over women and children.

For my mother it was the beginning of a very hard time. She was pregnant again and the baby was due in the middle of April! At the beginning of April my father's boss sent him home from Löbau in the Lausitz, to collect a colour-compressor from his workshop, to be used to camouflage military vehicles. Since this was so close to the end of the war, to this day we remain convinced that this was a humane gesture by his boss, who assumed that my father would use the opportunity to stay at home with his highly pregnant wife. However, conscientiously he returned to Löbau with the equipment. A car had come to collect him. What a difficult farewell for my mother – I can still remember the day vividly.

Now even we children noticed that things were getting serious; all adults were incredibly nervous; there were rumours of a 'wonder weapon', but my aunt from Berlin remained very sceptical, and destroyed our belief in its existence.

During the night of the fourteenth to fifteenth April, when Potsdam was carpet bombed, my mother went into labour. We were all in the air-raid shelter as the bomber planes flew in large formations above us bound for Potsdam. My poor mother was lying in the upper floor in the bedroom, but both her sisters were standing by her. Her youngest sister helped the little girl into this world. Later a midwife joined them and in the morning we could all admire our little sister. Everything had gone well and my mother luckily could breastfeed the baby and she survived.

We were getting more frightened every day, and we prepared to flee. Nappies and baby clothes filled our schoolbags, replacing our dolls. Fortunately we never had to leave our home.

On the second of May, 1945, Russians marched into Perleberg. The town was handed over without fighting. There apparently was a white flag hanging from the town hall. We sat in the cellar, fearfully awaiting further events. My grandfather was the only man with us. He had to box the ears of a young member of the Hitler Youth movement who wanted to leave the cellar to defend us in the street. Ten women and 14 children were now sitting and waiting in fear. Full of terror we watched as a fierce Mongolian descended the stairs, Kalashnikov at the ready, shouting 'URI-URI' (*watches-watches*). Trembling all over, all the women gave him their watches and jewellery. That was all he wanted.

In the evening we went upstairs into our flat and stayed together, forming a group for our protection and defence. The children were put to bed lying flat on the floor. Above in the attic were all the women. My grandfather was the children's guard. This turned out to be quite clever, because at night the Russians came back into the house. When they saw the numerous children and my grandfather, they shouted 'Ah, so many children!' and disappeared. The women upstairs were saved and so were we. Next morning one of the women tore up a sheet into strips, which we wound round our arms. This was supposed to mean: 'We have surrendered.' During the following days Russians marched continually into the town; in the evenings they searched the cellars and empty flats for booty. Besides clothing and cameras, a great number of jars filled with vividly dark red preserved strawberries disappeared from our cellar. My mother was full of *Schadenfreude* (*pleasure at the thieves' discomfort*). She had used too much colouring during the preserving and all the strawberries were bitter.

We children did not witness any brutalities, but many frightful scenes happened in the centre of Perleberg and several families took their own lives. Soon, some women were allowed to queue for bread near the barracks. In our cellar we still had a large quantity of butter left over from the store of the shop, which saved us in the first of our difficult periods. The wife of a wood-cutter made a soup of sorrel and nettles. All of the women were remarkably inventive in preparing meals.

My father returned home as early as mid-May 1945, together with a Polish man. Both were in rags, starving, but otherwise unhurt. My father had joined up with this fleeing Polish man. They had covered the whole distance, from Löbau in the

Lausitz to Perleberg, on foot or by hitching lifts. My father had pretended to be deaf and dumb and the Polish man could speak Russian. They must have had a guardian angel! The two men, to our great astonishment, ate a whole bucket full of boiled potatoes. Who knows what would have happened had my father become a deserter by hiding himself in April!

The other women had meanwhile returned to their own apartments. Now we four children once again had a father who could protect us and our mother. The Soviets called my father to their commander's headquarters in Perleberg to carry out painting work; he was renowned for his skill in painting cars. The commander had damaged his beautiful car while he was drunk and my father had repaired it expertly. Thereafter many other jobs came up. He was paid in foodstuffs, such as flour, sweets and once a goat. One night he arrived with a cow in tow! There was a meadow's edge nearby where she could have grazed, but she had to be taken to the slaughter-house, because she had foot and mouth disease. Our dream of fresh milk was gone.

To protect us from straying Russian soldiers, the commander gave a signed and stamped letter to my father, which declared that there was typhoid fever in our house. We hung the framed letter by the door and no Russian entered our house after that. They were very frightened of catching this disease.

In the summer of 1945 I had the chore of walking every evening, milk can in hand, the two miles to the next village to beg for milk for my little sister. But many other children and adults went on the same errand. We were not always successful. In the summer we harvested apples, pears and plums in our orchard. A part of this harvest was used for barter.

How lucky that my grandparents had planted such a lot of fruit trees after WWI! This soon taught us children how to help ourselves at a time of serious want.

One day someone brought a carton full of mouth organs, probably stolen. Fourteen children got two or three of them each and, of course, we all played them in the courtyard! Each played louder than the next. Our mothers must have had strong nerves!

From September 1945 onwards school re-started. Classes were huge, 50 to 60 pupils per class. There were very few teachers, because some of them had first to be de-Nazified (*a process introduced by the Allies to rid German and Austrian society of any remnants of National Socialist ideology*). I remember the cold winter of 1945/46. At home we all gathered together in one room during the daytime to keep warm. A small iron stove was our most important possession. The house had central heating but it had been turned off. When there was no electricity, homework had often to be done by candle light. In the evening we had to get into our ice-cold and clammy beds.

We now belonged to the Russian-occupied zone. Many people disappeared from our town after the end of the war; some were never seen again and their fate was never discovered. There were denunciations and a lot of suspicion amongst the population. Fear reigned again. Nevertheless, the survivors started to rebuild, though under great difficulties. My father soon reopened his business and most of his apprentices and skilled workmen returned to him. We children were particularly glad to see the return of one in particular, our much-loved Fritz. He remained faithfully working with my father past the 50-year anniversary of the start of the business, and is still alive today.

In the lessons at school in the GDR (*German Democratic Republic, i.e. East Germany*) we learned a lot about the Nazis and their brutalities. Resistance by the working class, especially by communists, was described in great detail in word and films. This led to discussions with our parents, who often doubted what we were reporting. The fathers kept silent about their experiences at the front during the war. We found out a lot later that there had been a civil resistance movement too.

During the continuing shortage of all goods in the GDR we all used the experience we had gained from the post-war years. Right to the end (*of the GDR*) in 1989 we had a society which survived through bartering goods.

One great wish was ever present: 'No war ever again!'

Ingrid's Memories

I was born in 1937 in Leipzig (see map 9 for main places mentioned in text), where we lived in a corner house with a large bay window. In this room my sister Christel and I were christened. When I was four years old I got my first box on the ears, which I still remember today: we had to go through the Jewish Quarter on our way to do some shopping. The Jews were not allowed to walk on the pavement but had to use the road, where they walked bent over and with the yellow star sewn on to their coats. In Kindergarten I had been taught that they were bad people! So I stuck out my tongue and made a face at them. My mother immediately boxed my ears. She told me that these were good people, but they were persecuted, and that in any case you were never allowed to behave like that towards adults.

During the war we moved to my grandparents' town of Naunhof, about 40 km from Leipzig, into a large apartment. Our garden, where we children always played, was close to my grandfather's. None of us had a watch so Hedwig, the cook, rang a large cow bell to make sure that we were punctual for meals. The neighbours' children had to go home then. All our meals were taken together with the whole family. The adults were very strict with us: we had to stand behind our chairs and wait until parents and grandparents were seated. Then we were allowed to sit down. When the adults talked we had to be silent.

In May 1941, my sister Andrea was born. Our nanny Elly looked after her. My great love was for our Airedale terrier, Falk, who had looked after me when I was in my pram in the garden. The war was getting worse and I was afraid of the burning houses. My grandmother and her sister had been bombed out of their house and could not rescue anything, so they came to live with us in Naunhof.

One day we were playing in our big sandpit. Next to us three geese were feeding. Suddenly I saw that all three geese had turned their heads towards the sky, all at the same time. I told my mother and we spotted a bomb, suspended on a parachute, sailing down onto the railway line. We immediately told the police, who stopped the train and dismantled the bomb. Our geese had prevented a catastrophe.

Apart from these geese we had chickens and rabbits, which were hidden from thieves in a shed. Although I loved wearing the warm gloves made of rabbit fur, I hated it when one of the rabbits had to be slaughtered. My grandfather was also a great beekeeper and had 12 beehives. The honeycombs full of honey were put into a hand-operated centrifuge, and the honey was poured straight into jars. At the end we little naked children were allowed to climb into the big centrifuge to lick out the last remains of honey, a feast for us! Since we were then very sticky all over, we were put into tin baths filled with rainwater warmed by the sun.

My father was called up and served as an officer in the navy in Cuxhaven. Air-raids started with low-flying planes, and sometimes in the middle of the night we had to run into the cellar. The next day, we collected the empty shells. Because there was all that shrapnel flying around, my grandfather built a bunker in the garden. Later he hid Jews in it, giving them money to escape from Germany.

The lawn was turned into vegetable beds. We learned early on how to grow vegetables and flowers in our own garden beds. Since manure could not easily be obtained we always had a wooden box and a shovel on our bikes to collect horse manure.

Many refugees passed through Naunhof in 1944 and we took Mrs Wohlang and her daughter Brigitte, who had come from Sudetenland (*the German-speaking areas of the former Czechoslovakia*), into our large apartment. From then on she cooked for us, and Brigitte, a year older than me, was like our fourth sister.

Gradually, there was no longer anything to buy, and food was rationed. Every now and then our grandparents exchanged jewellery and carpets with farmers for milk, flour and potatoes. Coal, soon only brown coal, was rationed too. The central heating could not be operated any longer. A wood-burning stove and a small tiled oven, which could also be fed with wood, were placed in the living room. We brought in coal every day and collected small pieces of wood in the forests. We took a little cart to the forest and brought out small tree trunks under covers, as only trunks up to a certain thickness were allowed to be taken from the forest. But soon, even that source of firewood became scarce as every family had the same idea.

Being the eldest, I went gleaning in the fields on the farm with my mother (later in the season we went to forage for potatoes on harvested fields). I had a little apron with a big pocket into which I could put the collected grain. This was quite hard work as the farmers did not leave very much on their fields after harvesting. The grain was stored in a small room in our attic. One day we discovered the key to this room and because we were always hungry, we ate the raw grain. My mother soon found out and we were boxed on the ears.

At Christmas we were given a pound of bread each, the best Christmas present we could have had. Later, every day after breakfast, each of us got half a slice of bread from our three grandparents, which made hunger a bit more bearable. There were no sweets, no chocolate, and no sugar. And since there were no new clothes and we kept growing, our grandmother sewed red and white dresses for us from the old Imperial flag. The black material in the flag was used to make gym shorts, which were very scratchy. On special days we had to hang out the swastika flags, but later they were used for making clothes as well. Grandmother was very modern: she had one of the first electric sewing machines but our own machine was powered by a foot treadle.

The worst time for us children was when, in 1943, Nanny Elly had to leave because we could no longer afford to pay her. Falk, our faithful dog, was taken away too and trained by mountain soldiers as an avalanche dog. Later we were told that he rescued many people. I cried for several days but my grandmother told me that he was much better off because we had nothing to feed him.

In the autumn of 1943 I started school. I proudly carried a leather schoolbag with a slate, slate-pencil and sponge. I was always teased as I was the tallest of the pupils.

I volunteered to harvest potatoes so that I could earn some money for the family. In the heat of the summer I also helped with carrot-harvesting in the fields. All schoolchildren also had to help by collecting potato beetles, which were a pest ruining potato harvests. In winter we often had no school for lack of electricity and heating. My grandmother gave lessons to us and to the neighbours' children. I especially liked geography, particularly when she told us of her travels and when she opened the large atlas of the world.

When the war finally ended in 1945, my father was in a British prisoner-of-war camp. As the American army arrived, we hurriedly hid our jewellery and silver cutlery under the bicycle shed, because we had heard rumours of plundering. We were very afraid but they were very nice people. Commander Liri chose my grandparents' house as his base and we all had to move out. We slept in another house, all in one large room full of strangers, only separated by a screen. My mother could speak a little English and managed to get permission from Liri to move the family, including our grandparents, back into our former apartment. But we were no longer allowed to go into our garden to harvest anything. The Americans threw away a great deal of their food and we collected a lot of edible stuff from their rubbish heap. Sometimes we begged outside the kitchen window and got some chocolate.

The Russian army was going to take over Saxony and Liri offered to take us and our furniture to West Germany or the USA. But where would my mother and her three children go to? It was also worrying that my father had not yet returned. All the women in our village were afraid of being raped by Russian soldiers. But somehow Liri managed to ensure that nobody came to any harm in our village of Naunhof. As the American soldiers had moved things from houses all over the village, people began frantically searching for their belongings. Everybody brought anything that did not belong to them to the market-place and in this way we got back most of our furniture, linen, laundry and clothes.

Lessons in Russian started now at school. We had very young, new teachers. The Young Pioneers' movement was started. Church attendance was frowned upon. Instead of confirmation the so-called youth consecration was introduced (*Jugendweihe was a secular ceremony for all 14-year-olds)*. We tried to avoid most of these Communist practices.

In 1948 our father came back from his prisoner-of-war camp. He went first to friends in West Germany to regain some weight and then moved to Bielefeld (*in West Germany*), where a lot of our relatives lived. He earned some money working on building sites and selling mushrooms to delicatessen shops. He had to be denazified. My father was never a Nazi but had to join the party, otherwise he would not have been able to open a barrister's office. As often as he could, he visited us in East Germany illegally. He told us stories that on these trips he experienced more danger than during the entire war and that he was chased by dogs and could only find the right direction by following the pole star.

Having been a barrister, he was on the list to be sent to a Siberian labour camp, and for this reason nobody was allowed to know of his visits to us. Mostly, he signalled his arrival in the dark whistling a certain birdcall. He could never let us know when he would visit. Once, when he was with us, he helped to collect wood and put on my mother's dress. My grandfather wanted to give this helpful 'lady' five Deutschmarks; he had not recognised his son-in-law! My father was often caught crossing the border but somehow always managed to get free again. If he got caught on the way to us, he did not bring us any food, as it was taken away from him. He let us know of his safe return by sending coded postcards. One day somebody must have given him away. When the police came, my father hid underneath the writing desk, which had a back panel. He was very slim and the big waste paper basket was enough to hide him. This incident prompted my father to try to get us out and over to the West.

Next time he arrived with a special pass, which, with the help of relatives, 'attested' that he had already lived in Bielefeld (*in West Germany*) before the war. We added the name of my little sister Andrea, onto the pass, which luckily no one noticed. She arrived in Bielefeld with my father but soon after fell ill with tuberculosis. A worrying time began for my parents, but Andrea was well looked after in the children's hospital.

My mother crossed the border into West Germany, near Wolfenbüttel, illegally: first with my sister Christel, and later with me. I remember that we got caught by Russian soldiers. I took my teddy bear and a puppet from the top of my knapsack into my arms and cried bitterly. The children-loving Russians let us go. It was rather foggy and my mother found a young man who took us, for money, through the forest to the border. We got very precise instructions about when the patrols were passing and hid in a bush. When everything was clear we reached the free West. In Hanover my mother put me onto a train to Munich. She had to farm out her children in preparation for the move to West Germany. Friends of my grandmother had been told to expect me at the station in Munich; they had a white candle in their hands and took me kindly into their arms. As a first meal they gave me pasta, my favourite meal. I ate half a pound of it all by myself, because I was so hungry and, of course, I had to stay in bed the next day with a sore stomach. The four-week stay turned into six months.

My father had rented a wooden house in Bielefeld in 1951 where he planned to reunite the family. But this house had been built illegally and, since a road was planned there, the house had to be pulled down. We would have had to go into a refugee camp in Friedland. However, my grandfather's youngest sister moved in with her daughter and let us have her apartment.

This was the beginning of another difficult time for my parents and I really admired how they managed everything. The flat was at ground level and consisted of a large room with dark wine-red wallpaper. A conservatory had been built onto it and made it so dark that we had to turn on electric lights even during the day. Another family and a journalist also lived in this flat. There was just one toilet and one kitchen. There was no running water in our room and we had to wash in a bowl and use a large carafe for water. Once a week we went to the public baths. Christel slept on a sofa, I on a camp bed in the cold conservatory and our parents in a bed. For one year everything took place in this one room. I got an ear infection every three months and my mother's rheumatoid arthritis started.

As malnourished children, Christel and I were both sent (*through a programme of sending needy children into the country to recover*) to Wangerooge (*an island in the North Sea*). Afterwards, I started at a gymnasium (*secondary school)* but had great problems with languages. I had missed the introduction to English and never really caught up. Andrea caused us a lot of anxiety as she had to spend a long time in hospital and had to have several operations.

In 1952 the town council gave us a flat on the edge of Bielefeld with three very small rooms, but we had a bathroom and a kitchen to ourselves and were a happy family. Later we obtained a permit to legally move our furniture from Naunhof to Bielefeld. Silver and valuable porcelain was not allowed to be taken out of East Germany. Two years later we moved again, this time into a very beautiful three-roomed apartment on the first floor - with a garden. Slowly our lives improved. My father became a commercial representative. However, my mother's arthritis got much worse and, although she tried all sorts of cures and therapies, nothing really helped. In 1955 I passed my O-levels. My dream was to be a physiotherapist for which there was, however, a four-year waiting list. So I decided to train as a medical-technical assistant.

Throughout these years, the security within my family has given me strength to survive all the experiences of my wartime childhood and for this I am eternally grateful.

Joachim's Memories

*That's how it was then . . . .   that's how Joachim experienced
the end of the war and the time after it.*

On that day, the fourth of March, 1945, the little county town
of Greifenberg in Pomerania (see map 10 for main places
mentioned in text) lay in wintry quiet, covered by deep snow
which had lain there for several weeks. It was a deceptive calm
which increasingly developed into anxious unrest. A line of
refugees with many horse-drawn carriages passed through the
Königstrasse towards the west. Military convoys travelled in
the opposite direction towards the east and the front line. The
thunder of heavy artillery came ever closer, at first just a
distant rumble which grew louder, until the impacts of
individual shells could be heard more and more clearly. At
night, we children were frightened by the flash of the
explosions and we hid deep under the blankets.

On that day, the fourth of March, 1945, a Sunday, women and
children were commanded to evacuate their homes. Many
people from Greifenberg left the town and we went to the
railway station. My family group consisted of my mother, me
(ten and a half years old), and three cousins. They had fled with
their mother from Königsberg in East Prussia. A military
aeroplane had taken them out of the besieged town but it
crashed due to engine trouble near Kohlberg in Pomerania. My
aunt was lying in hospital, seriously injured, and we had taken
in the little ones. They were eight, six and three years old.

My 19-year-old sister had to remain in Greifenberg. She had
been drafted into service at the post office and was not allowed
to leave the town. At the station there was chaos. The main

railway was allowed to take only refugees from the front line and soldiers. People from Greifenberg were directed to take the narrow-gauge railway. Each of us carried a small knapsack containing just the bare necessities. The few railway carriages for passengers on our train were already full. We climbed into an open-topped freight wagon and sat there freezing on the bare floor waiting for our departure.

On the platform there were some onlookers who still believed in a final victory for Germany. I remember an acquaintance who shouted to my mother: 'What, are you leaving too? We are staying here! This morning, we heard on the radio that the Führer is going to use his wonder weapon now and then the enemy will be destroyed!' I wonder what happened to this lady when the town went up in flames the next day and was overrun by the Red Army.

There were many dead among the civilian population. We lost six family members: the youngest was just 15. However, we were lucky; our train finally got moving with a lot of puffing. We said good bye to Greifenberg, not knowing that it would be forever.

During a heavy snowstorm and in icy temperatures we arrived at Ziegendorf, a village on the Stettiner Haff *(a large bay in the Baltic Sea)*. We spent the night together with many other refugees on the bare wooden floor of the 'Dorfkrug' *(the village pub)*. The next morning a small steamboat took us to the other side of the Haff to Stepenitz. This was nearly our last journey! A Russian fighter plane attacked the steamer, until a German fighter plane attacked it in turn and chased it away.

From Stepenitz to Stettin was not very far. At the main railway station we were pushed into an already overcrowded train. Soldiers lifted the children through the windows. We were glad to be able to leave the town quickly as it was bombarded almost every night.

After several days' travelling, we finally reached our goal: the town of Tangermünde. We had some relatives living here who were expecting us. My uncle was the commercial director of the Tangermünde sugar and chocolate factory and lived with his family in a spacious villa where there was room for us as well. A fortnight later my sister, whom we had to leave behind in Greifenberg, arrived there too. She had left Greifenberg on the same day as we did on the very last narrow-gauge train.

After a further two weeks the war caught up with us in Tangermünde but this time from the west. American troops were stationed just outside the town. Even though there had been no bombardment of the town, rumoured to be because English capital was invested in the sugar factory, we had to be prepared for battle action to come. A few tank barriers in the road made us suspect that it was imminent. The factory headquarters had therefore arranged for horse-drawn carriages to take women and children into one of the nearby villages, to await events in safety. We were allowed to travel with them.

The first contact with the 'enemy' was not long in coming. In a wooded area an American tank unit was suddenly seen rolling towards our column of carriages. On top of the tanks, captured German soldiers were sitting, acting as living shields! Quite clever, those Americans! Who would shoot their own comrades? We were not run over and finally arrived in a nearby village, where we were given shelter in barns.

On top of the church tower a farmer was keeping the country road under observation through his binoculars. Whenever enemy units were approaching he hung a white sheet from the window of the tower as a sign of surrender. If, however, German troops were approaching, the sheet was hauled in quickly and exchanged for a flag with the swastika on it. There was, after all, the death sentence for surrender, and German military police, also called 'watch dogs', knew no mercy. They strung up many a person on the next lamp-post. There were several changes of flags on the church tower on that day.

At last, messengers brought the news that we should return. American troops had occupied Tangermünde. When our horse-drawn carriages drove into the town, passers-by bombarded us with sweets. The chocolate factory had been ransacked. Many of the inhabitants had helped themselves to a lot of sweets, sugar and flavourings. These were desirable goods for exchange! We children particularly liked the *'Nährstangen'* a special sweet made only in Tangermünde, which can still be bought there today.

Fortunately, there were no real battles in Tangermünde. After the German troops had retreated across the bridge over the River Elbe towards the east, blowing up the bridge behind them, the few *'Volkssturm'* pensioners *(towards the end of the war, 15-year-olds and pensioners were given weapons and told to defend the bridges)* who had been left in the town offered no resistance to the Americans. Only a few fanatical Hitler youths, still half children, insisted on playing the hero. They fired with anti-tank hand guns from a cellar window at the passing tanks. The boys were quickly caught and executed without mercy.

We had just settled ourselves in my uncle's villa when a command from the Americans reached all inhabitants to evacuate the town again. Nobody knew why! So we moved to the village of Heeren, which was 7 km away. About 6,000 people from Tangermünde were there already, a dense throng of people. We were quartered in a farmhouse where there were already 130 people. Nearly a week passed before we were allowed to return to Tangermünde.

Many houses and flats had been plundered and laid waste. In the sugar factory there had been a prisoner-of-war camp with Russians and Poles, who had to work there. These men had been set free and had taken the opportunity to recompense themselves for their forced labour. Occupying force members were also involved. I saw a coloured American soldier who had at least five watches on each of his forearms which he showed off proudly. In my uncle's villa there was now an army hospital and so we had to find somewhere else to live.

After some time, the Americans left. Canadian units came and they in turn were replaced by British troops.

At Yalta, Germany's opponents *(the 'Big Three' powers, USA, UK and Russia met at Yalta in February 1945, for a conference)* had agreed that the Western Allied troops should advance only to the River Elbe. The Red Army therefore had to move its front west to the Elbe. The English army waited in Tangermünde. In the afternoons, for 'five o'clock tea', their tanks drove up to the top of a vineyard and fired shots for about half an hour across the Elbe into the remaining German units. These units did not mount any resistance and withdrew from the meadows into the woods. One day there was an embarrassing incident. Once again the 'Tommies', as we called the English, shot across the river at moving military vehicles. However, they were not Germans but Russians, who were not at all amused by it and angrily returned fire. Unfortunately things like this do happen every now and then in the heat of battle. Incidentally, these shots fired in Tangermünde were the last shots of the war in Europe.

At Yalta it had also been decided that large areas west of the Elbe should be handed over to the Russian occupying army. In exchange for this it was agreed that the Western Allies were to occupy part of Berlin. The German capital city, which had been conquered by the Russians, thus became a four-sector city.

For Tangermünde this meant yet another change of occupying forces. The English moved out and the Russians took over the town. We Germans were none too happy about this. The women in particular had to be vigilant. Again and again rape was committed, even though Russian officers sometimes took strict measures and punished the perpetrators. I myself saw how a 'Muschkote', as we called the ordinary Russian soldiers, was beaten so severely by a Russian officer that he ended up in hospital.

For us boys from Tangermünde this was the beginning of an exciting time. The Russians built a wooden bridge right next to the old bridge across the Elbe, which had been destroyed. Germans were allowed to cross it as well. After school we were always attracted to the other side of the Elbe. There, the German army had dumped huge amounts of war machinery and ammunition. It was strictly forbidden to touch these things, let alone to play with them, but who was going to observe that prohibition? A lot of fish can be caught by throwing hand grenades into rivers and lakes. They provided a welcome addition to our otherwise rather meagre diet.

We did not like shooting with rifles quite as much, as the rebound of the rifle left hefty bruises on our shoulders. However, with pistols we had many a shoot-out contest. Gunpowder, which could be used for many purposes, was very much in demand. We obtained it from high-explosive shells, whose explosive charge was carefully poured out. Grinning, we would smuggle the contraband hidden in our school bags past the Russian guards on the bridge over the Elbe. It was obvious that this dangerous play could go awry. Several pupils were badly injured and one even lost his life. Finally this macabre pastime stopped. Common sense prevailed upon even the most courageous dare-devil.

The biggest problem of this time was constant hunger. The meagre rations obtainable with the ration cards were not sufficient to fill up hungry, growing children. Often, we had to go to bed with rumbling stomachs. For my eleventh birthday I had just one wish: to eat my fill of bread! We had to become self-reliant. Grain was collected from harvested fields and any remaining potatoes were dug up. Tasty salads and soups were made from dandelion, nettle and sorrel leaves.

Then there was the illegal acquisition of food supplies: from orchards we stole apples, pears and berries. You had to be very careful not to be caught by the guards. They thrashed thieves mercilessly. In the autumn, tons of sugar beet was transported to the factory for processing. Many horse-drawn carts were driven along the roads, heaped to the top with sugar beet. Of course, this reawakened our longing for sugar. The fittest of us jumped onto the backs of the carts, holding on with one hand and with the other hand threw as many as they could down on to the road, until they lost their grip. The boys following on foot collected the booty. Everything had to be done very quickly, so that the driver did not notice anything. At home our mothers did not ask where the sugar beet had come from. Quietly, they were used up.

When the winter of 1945-46 was approaching – it was going to be a very cold winter – enough fuel had to be found. The little coal which was supplied was not enough to keep even one room heated. In the surrounding woods many people were busy collecting sacks full of pine cones. All the branches lying around were collected; laboriously, people took out tree roots by hand, and when the forester was not looking several small trees were quickly cut down. Afterwards the forest looked swept clean. Mountains of coal were stored on the areas belonging to the railway, which were guarded by Russians. Here too, the boys had a plan: girls were sent out as decoys; they went up to the guards and flirted with them to distract them. That was the moment when we crept up from the other side and quickly pinched some coal. Necessity is the mother of invention.

Slowly, life became more normal. Our father, who had been stationed as a soldier in Denmark, was released from a British prison-of-war camp at the end of 1946 and returned to us. Our family was happily reunited.

After finishing school, my time in Tangermünde came to an end. Occupational choice led to a move to another town, until finally in 1960 I made my new home in Berlin.

I enjoy thinking back to the beautiful old town of Tangermünde on the Elbe, which became my second home, after I lost my first one. Everyone has their own definition of 'home' (*Heimat*). The older generation can only accept the town in which they were born and grew up as 'home'. My parents belonged to this generation. They never felt at home in Tangermünde and could not accept that they were exiled for ever from their beloved Greifenberg in Pomerania, where for more than 700 years their German forefathers had lived. Younger people define the word *Heimat* more freely. For them home is wherever they feel well, where they are happy and where they feel safe. I belong to this group.

Renate's Memories

When, in 1938, I was born the second child of my parents – my brother was just one year old – in a south-eastern suburb of Berlin (see map 11 for main places mentioned in text), war had not yet started, but at the same time Germany was not really at peace. Nevertheless, the first years of my life were safe and carefree. We played in our small garden and my brother and I were inseparable, like twins.

My parents were not followers of Hitler, let alone Nazis – my father came from a social-democratic working-class family with many children and had worked hard to become a secondary school teacher of English and German. However, they were not in the resistance either. What sort of hero would one have to be with two, later three, small children to risk that?

In 1941 my father was transferred to the Goethe Gymnasium in Landsberg on the river Warthe – which is on the other side of the river Oder, today Gorzow in Poland. In 1943 he was called up to the front in the West. In 1944 my sister was born during an air-raid; she was a so-called *Fronturlaubskind* (*a child conceived during a soldier's home-leave from the front*). Even as a new-born she had to go hungry, because my mother was emaciated. We were, nevertheless, lucky because a neighbour took us with him on his lorry to Berlin in January 1945, with the Russian army so close behind us that we could hear the heavy artillery. We, that is my mother, two children seven and six years old, a ten-month-old baby and my 80-year-old grandfather, escaped with only our lives. I can't precisely remember, but at that time there must still have been bridges across the Oder which were later blown up. I do remember, however, seeing burning tanks and dead people along the way.

On arrival in Berlin, we were at first taken in by my grandmother in Berlin-Wedding, into a large apartment on the fourth floor of a block of flats. It was very crowded as numerous aunts and cousins from my father's large family had also taken shelter there.

If you wanted to find out the truth about the situation on the battle fronts, you had to search for the 'tum tum station' on your wireless, the BBC (which was, of course, strictly forbidden), recognisable by the beginning of Beethoven's Fifth Symphony which they transmitted at constantly changing frequencies. Ta-ta-ta-taaa ... this is how my mother found out about the real state of the war.

In the spring of 1945 the air-battle raged above Berlin. Every night we were violently wakened from sleep and taken to air-raid shelters, bare, grey rooms, where we sat, frightened, hearing and feeling every explosion as the bombs hit their targets around us. Even today, I can't hear a siren without remembering the bombs and the air-raid shelter. One night the front of our house was destroyed by a bomb, including my grandmother's bedroom. She promptly barricaded the door to the bedroom so that nobody would step through it into empty space and fall down four floors to the ground. For lack of space we could no longer stay there and had to move on to relatives of my mother's in a villa in the previously elegant suburb of Berlin-Schlachtensee. They were still a well-to-do family, who asked for our children's ration cards for their single son as 'rent'. This is how you find out people's true characters! My father later broke off any contact with these relatives.

At Schlachtensee we experienced the final battle for Berlin. First the Russians arrived, then the Americans. I have two clear memories of this time. Once, a Russian soldier had already lined us up against the wall by drawing his machine-gun so that he could search us for watches and jewellery, when a Russian officer arrived who was friendly and loved children and put an end to this ordeal. He even gave us biscuits! This was an unimaginable treat for us half-starved children with swollen bellies, because at this time we were fed on 'nettle-spinach' and potato peelings, which my mother collected from strangers' dustbins and made into a kind of pancake. On the other hand, I remember an event when the Americans were stationed in the neighbouring villa. A very tall, black American soldier deliberately poured the bean soup from his mess tin into the sand on the other side of the fence in front of my hungry eyes. Propaganda works everywhere – years after the end of the war, as a direct consequence of the German war propaganda, I dreamed that I was sitting on the staircase to the cellar and the Russians arrived and hacked me into pieces.

My mother told me later how she was chased off a farmyard near Berlin by dogs when she tried to exchange her last 'beautiful' dress for something to eat. Farmers had, at that time, hoarded many valuables which people had bartered for food, but we did not have anything left to exchange. My mother told me that her eyes had nearly popped out when the farmer's wife had even put meat into their dog's food bowl.

The winter of 1945/46 was particularly cold. We could not obtain any fuel, so my sister and brother and I had big chilblains on our hands and feet. The church had given us second-hand shoes, which did not, however, fit us. We wound pieces of cloth around our feet and somehow my mother had found some cream of camphor, which helped a little.

We lived through the division of Berlin into four sectors, which were given to the four victorious allies: the USA, Russia, Great Britain and France. It was a lucky chance that we lived in a part of the city which was now part of West Berlin. Another lucky chance was that my father had been interred in a British prisoner-of-war camp, where he was able to work as an interpreter. He came home in 1947 and my little sister, who did not recognise him, said, 'Look there comes Uncle Willy' when he came through the door. Since my father had not been a member of the NS (*National Socialist Party*) and thus had a clear record, he was taken back into the education service.

We lived through the currency reform and, during the Cold War, through the Blockade of Berlin by the Russians, which the Western Allies broke through with their Airlift in June 1948 to May 1949. Unfortunately, there were several casualties among the pilots. The people of Berlin affectionately called the aeroplanes *Rosinenbomber* (*raisin bombers*), because they dropped off parcels of food. If I close my eyes, I can still taste the dried carrots and 'pom', the mashed potatoes. The monument to the Airlift, which the city of Berlin later erected in memory of the pilots and the victims at the airport of Tempelhof, and which is called 'Hunger Fork'(*Hungergabel*) by the inhabitants of Berlin, still reminds us of that time.

We eventually got our own flat and school started again. My brother and I were put straight away into the third and second class respectively, because my mother had taught us herself during the last phases of the war and afterwards. We could read and write and do our sums, but, like most other children, we were disturbed and did things which we certainly would not have done without the influence of the war. I remember that I once found a blue chiffon scarf which, of course, I should not have taken away with me. But I took it home, because I wanted to give my mother some pleasure. Of course, I was questioned and had to take the scarf back the next day. Was I now a thief?

My father smoked a pipe and that is why he grew tobacco, as well as tomatoes, on the balcony. We children collected horse manure and got five pennies as a reward. Pine cones were collected to be burnt in the stove and sometimes we were lucky and could brush up some coal dust when a coal lorry had passed by.

My father had formed a friendship with a Professor Picton when he studied under him in London before the war. Through him I got an English pen friend when I was first learning the English language. When in 1953 my father became director of a Gymnasium (*secondary school*) his school was twinned with Nunthorpe Grammar School in Yorkshire, England, and we received exchange pupils from there. I have kept my father's English books with me all my life.

The German economic miracle started. My parents, though, had to start at zero and for several years after the war I had to wear hand-me-downs from my mother, which she altered for me. Sometimes, when my classmates teased me about my unfashionable clothes, I was ashamed. However, it slowly got better, and I finished school with the *Abitur (A-levels)* in 1956, aged 17, and could go straight to a technical college. In 1958 I started to work.

At last, discussions about the Nazi regime started in Germany. I cannot remember that we ever talked about the Third Reich in our lessons at school. Somehow, history always ended with Napoleon and Bismarck. I did not consciously follow the Nuremberg trials, and people resolutely expunged the Nazi period from their memories and kept silent about what had happened; all were busy rebuilding their lives (and, I hope, also coping with shock and shame). However, at the beginning of the 1960s the first legal processes against the Nazi criminals took place and the things that were reported in newspapers about those people seemed totally unimaginable. Then I started to look around and asked myself what they did, what they knew and what they should or could have known. My childhood view expanded from the terror of war with hunger, freezing and fear to the guilt of our people, and I struggled with my identity as a German. Shame and guilt are often still with me today.

Rolf's Memories

Soon after I was born in Munich (see map 12 for main places mentioned in text) in 1937 we moved to Starnberg in Bavaria. When I was about four or five years old my mother travelled with me to Berlin to visit her sister. One of my first memories is of a big air-raid on Berlin. We spent our first and only night in Berlin in a cellar. Next morning we started immediately on our journey back home. We walked towards the station through streets which were covered with rubble between the remaining façades of houses. The biggest pieces of rubble were lying in the middle of the road and covered it so completely that it was no longer visible. The smaller pieces of house walls were lying on top. We walked for a long time through this ghostly landscape of destruction on our way to the station.

When I started school it was expected of us that we should start the school day with the German Leader's greeting 'Heil Hitler'. Since I was clearly not brought up 'in the right way' I raised the wrong, my left, arm for the greeting. This would have meant trouble with a teacher who was a true Nazi as it would have led to the conclusion that my family did not conform to the party line. Luckily, my teacher overlooked my mistake and there were no consequences.

When an air-raid killed many people in Starnberg, my mother decided to move to our house in Eichstätt in the valley of the River Altmühl. This town seemed to have been spared air-raids since there was a prisoner-of-war camp for English officers. My father's textile factory was in Eichstätt; he was not a party member but nevertheless had been called up before the beginning of the war to march with the army into Austria. The production in the factory had to be changed to make uniforms. The management of the factory was given to a party member, who later, when my father was away for a long time in a French prisoner-of-war camp, appropriated the factory for himself.

My mother regularly listened to the BBC on the wireless. The use of this source of information, announced by the well-known Beethoven tune da-da-da-dum was risky and could have led to the death penalty. For this reason my mother let our shepherd dog out into our big garden so that, since our house was the last one up on the hill, he would have warned us of any approaching eavesdropper.

From the position of our house above the valley of the Altmühl we could, in the summer of 1944, watch the Allied bomber planes flying in huge numbers in the direction of Munich. Almost every day they flew in formations of four by four for about two hours above us. I can still vividly remember these shining silver bombers in the blue sky.

During one of the last days of the war the British prisoner-of-war officers were to have been moved. The apparently excellent information of the Allies had found out that the camp was to be emptied at seven in the morning. However, some delays led to a late departure of the prisoners-of-war. Low-flying British fighter planes discovered the marching columns and shot at them, not realising that they were killing hundreds of their own people.

From our house we had a good view of the bridge over the Altmühl and the avenue leading towards it. The bridge had been blown up in the last days of the war and we could watch the American tanks crossing the shallow river, albeit slowly, but without difficulties, driving on top of the ruins of the bridge. On the trees of the avenue two citizens of Eichstätt had been strung up by the SS; they had flown white flags, signifying surrender, from their windows a few hours too early.

Our house was commandeered straight away by the Americans and we carried a few basic belongings to friendly neighbours who took us in. However, after a few days we were allowed to return to the basement of our house. My mother was hired for translation and for cooking. Every now and then some of the food was left for us and since we were allowed to carry on working in our garden we didn't suffer from hunger. We also kept chickens, whose eggs were in great demand by the Americans. A black soldier called 'Soapy' liked to exchange fresh eggs for tinned food and chocolate. It was from him that I also got my first banana.

One evening the doorbell rang and my mother was told to open the door. Behind her several of 'our Americans' were positioned, pistols at the ready, as they still feared armed Germans on the run. But it was only a young German woman, who had become bored waiting outside for her American boyfriend!

When my father, who was at this time in Russia, realised that the end of the war was very near, he made his way towards the West with the aim of being taken prisoner by the Americans. After about two weeks of walking at night he achieved that aim, but the Americans immediately handed him over to the French. There he had to carry out heavy work in the forests with minimal nourishment. After the prison-of-war camps were disbanded, he remained in France and later, my parents having got divorced, married a French woman. I saw him again only when I was 15 years old. Neither then nor during later, rare meetings did we ever talk about the war.

Roswitha's Memories

I was born in Eichberg in the district of Bunzlau, Silesia (see map 13 for main places mentioned in text) on 26. December 1937. I was a premature, six-month baby and it was a great achievement for my mother to have brought me through the winter of 1937. The nearest children's hospital with the equipment necessary for premature babies weighing just 1,300 grams at birth was unreachable in the hard winter of 1937. My mother had not in the least expected to give birth at this early date and for this reason there were no baby's clothes or other useful items, such as baby's bottles, in our household. My brother - older than me by two and a half years – and I grew up on my father's family estate. My father drove into the nearest town and bought baby clothes and a toy baby's bottle with which my mother fed me drop by drop as soon as I was awake.

In spite of my early birth I had a normal childhood on our estate. I started school at five, a year earlier than is usual (*the normal age for starting school in Germany is six*), at our village school because I was found occupying myself with my brother's homework. At the school, three age groups were taught together in one classroom. Soon lessons became more and more sporadic, then the teacher from the neighbouring village took over the lessons and, when he was called up for army service, classes ceased altogether.

Up to this time we had not been touched by the war. However, when the first refugees from provinces further to the east passed through our village, and when my father was also called up for military service, we did have direct experience of the changes brought on by the war.

In February 1945, my mother with my brother and me and her in-laws started our flight (from the advancing Russian army) with three horse-drawn carriages. On the second day my grandmother died from a lung embolism. This was my first experience of death. We continued our flight after her burial. We never joined the mass trek of refugees but always kept more or less to ourselves, though supported by the large circle of my grandfather's acquaintances. Everywhere we found shelter for ourselves and the animals until the animals contracted foot-and-mouth disease and stopped our journey at Hoyerswerda, northeast of Dresden. After six weeks of waiting for the veterinary office to allow the animals to travel on, we continued north in the direction of Brandenburg, where a cousin of my grandfather's and his wife owned a large estate. My grandfather thought that we would have everything we needed there. He did not expect the Russian army to catch up with us there. But that is exactly what happened in April 1945. However, my mother had felt that staying in the country was too unsafe. For this reason she had moved with my brother and me to the next county town, Wittstock on the River Dosse. One of my father's cousins lived there and he took us in. It was here that I had the following experience:

My father's cousin had a big garden where he grew blackcurrants. My mother, my brother and I helped pick the berries. On one of these days, I quarrelled with my brother and eventually started to cry. At this moment a Russian soldier approached us and gave us to understand that we should wait there for him. After a short time he returned and gave me a whole loaf of army bread, stroked my head and indicated to my brother that he should not quarrel with me again. Then he walked away. My mother, who had observed the scene, joined us and with a big smile I gave her the loaf of bread. Russian soldiers were known to be very child-friendly; only the Mongolian soldiers were not very popular with us children. Perhaps it was their slit-eyes that frightened us? I never had direct contact with them.

We had not heard from my father since the winter of 1944. But my mother had continuously sent news to him of our flight. She always sent him open postcards addressed to his field post number.

In August 1945, schools in the former Soviet-occupied zone reopened and I was put into the third year class. In September 1945 my mother shared her secret plan with my brother and me, telling us that we would attempt an escape at night into Lower Saxony, crossing the River Ohre, a subsidiary of the River Elbe. Thus it happened that the three of us crossed the border illegally into the part of Germany which was occupied by the Western Allies. My grandfather did not come with us as he still hoped to return one day to Silesia. Up to his death in 1953 he still added to his address the comment: 'at present'.

After eight days, during which my mother, my brother and I were channelled through various refugee camps in Hamburg, we reached my maternal grandparents, carrying only one small rucksack. We had started our flight on three horse-drawn carriages packed with all our goods and chattels. All that was left now fitted into a single rucksack.

But the best thing was that, eight days after us, my father arrived in Hamburg from his imprisonment in Russia. He had suspected that we would have ended up with his parents-in-law. He had received all the postcards my mother had sent to him in the field and thus knew that his mother had died during the flight and that there was no longer a Silesia for him.

Notes for English readers for the following 13 maps of Germany, which was partitioned into zones in 1945.

A = American Zone

B = British Zone

F = French Zone

S = Soviet Zone

P = under Polish Administration

R = under Soviet Administration

The numbers within these zones refer to the main places mentioned in the relevant English and German texts.

The following maps refer to the main places mentioned in the following chapters:

Map 1 - Karte 1: Anne's Memories - Annes Erinnerungen

Map 2 – Karte 2: Barbara's Memories - Barbaras Erinnerungen

Map 3 – Karte 3: Bärbel's Memories - Bärbels Erinnerungen

Map 4 - Karte 4: Christine's Memories - Christines Erinnerungen

Map 5 - Karte 5: Dörthe's Memories - Dörthes Erinnerungen

Map 6 – Karte 6: Erika's Memories - Erikas Erinnerungen

91

Map 7 – Karte 7: Helga's Memories - Helgas Erinnerungen

Map 8 - Karte 8: Henriette's Memories - Henriettes Erinnerugnen

Map 9 - Karte 9: Ingrid's Memories - Ingrids Erinnerungen

Map 10 - Karte 10: Joachim's Memories - Joachims Erinnerungen

Map 11 - Karte 11: Renate's Memories - Renates Erinnerungen

Map 12 - Karte 12: Rolf's Memories - Rolfs Erinnerungen

Map 13 – Karte 13: Roswitha's Memories - Roswithas Erinnerungen

The maps are after 'www.unser-reich.info/images/ganzes-reich'

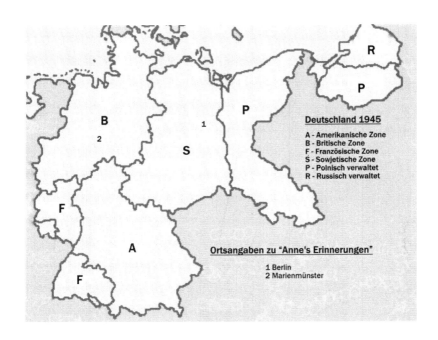

Deutschland 1945

A - Amerikanische Zone
B - Britische Zone
F - Französische Zone
S - Sowjetische Zone
P - Polnisch verwaltet
R - Russisch verwaltet

Ortsangaben zu "Anne's Erinnerungen"

1 Berlin
2 Marienmünster

Map 1 – Karte 1

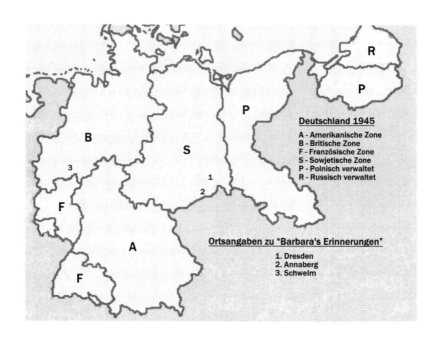

Map 2 – Karte 2

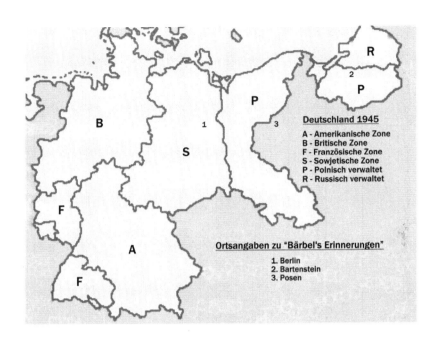

Map 3 – Karte 3

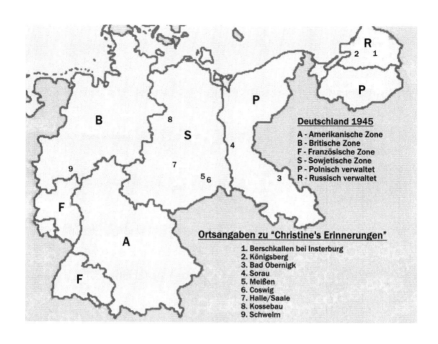

Map 4 – Karte 4

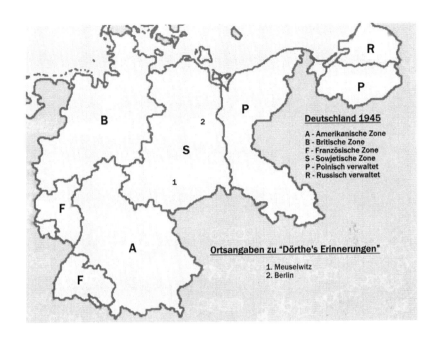

Deutschland 1945

A - Amerikanische Zone
B - Britische Zone
F - Französische Zone
S - Sowjetische Zone
P - Polnisch verwaltet
R - Russisch verwaltet

Ortsangaben zu "Dörthe's Erinnerungen"

1. Meuselwitz
2. Berlin

Map5 – Karte 5

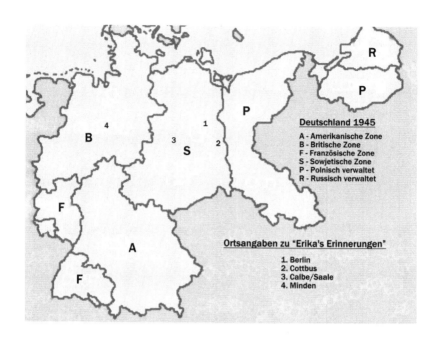

Map 6 – Karte 6

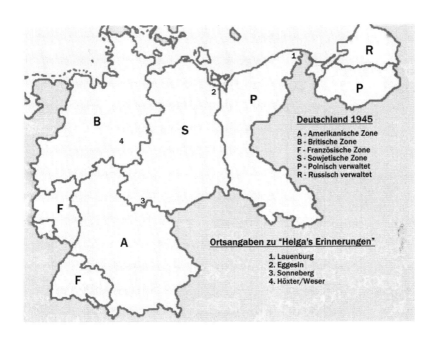

Map7 – Karte 7

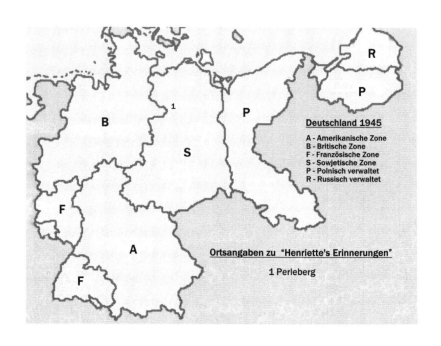

Deutschland 1945

A - Amerikanische Zone
B - Britische Zone
F - Französische Zone
S - Sowjetische Zone
P - Polnisch verwaltet
R - Russisch verwaltet

Ortsangaben zu "Henriette's Erinnerungen"

1 Perleberg

Map 8 – Karte 8

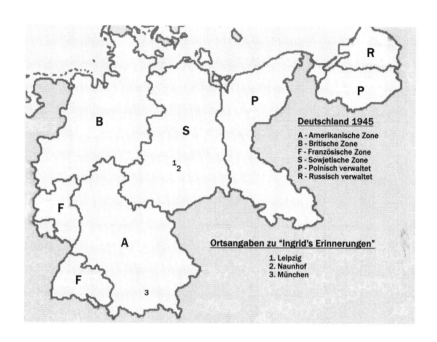

Deutschland 1945

A - Amerikanische Zone
B - Britische Zone
F - Französische Zone
S - Sowjetische Zone
P - Polnisch verwaltet
R - Russisch verwaltet

Ortsangaben zu "Ingrid's Erinnerungen"

1. Leipzig
2. Naunhof
3. München

Map 9 – Karte 9

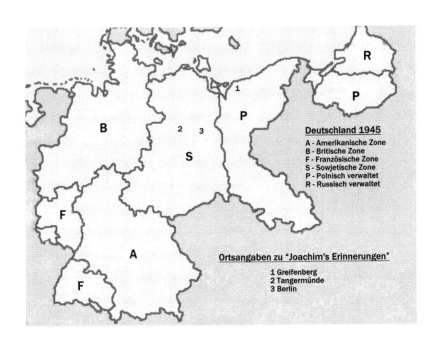

Map 10 – Karte 10

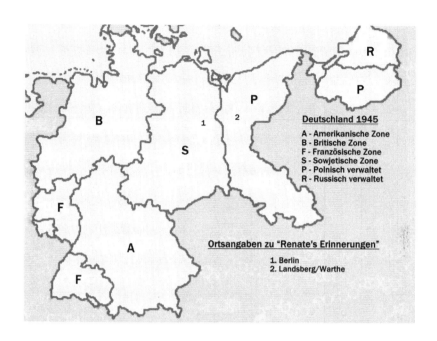

Deutschland 1945

A - Amerikanische Zone
B - Britische Zone
F - Französische Zone
S - Sowjetische Zone
P - Polnisch verwaltet
R - Russisch verwaltet

Ortsangaben zu "Renate's Erinnerungen"

1. Berlin
2. Landsberg/Warthe

Map 11 – Karte 11

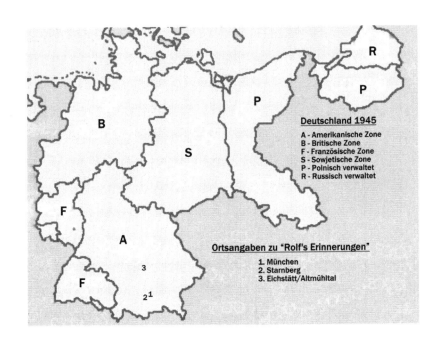

Map 12 – Karte 12

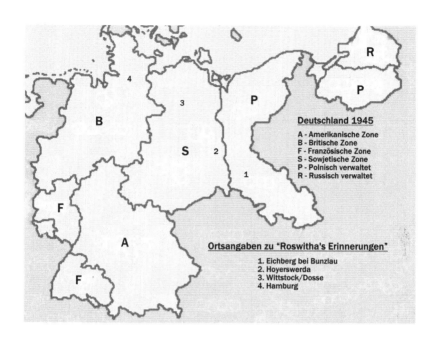

Map 13 – Karte 13

VORWORT

Erinnerungen an meine Kindheit im Zweiten Weltkrieg in Deutschland waren mir in den vergangenen Jahrzehnten immer wieder einmal durch den Kopf gegangen: Sätze – kurze Abschnitte – unzusammenhängende Geschehnisse – Erinnerungen wach gerufen durch Dokumentationen oder Filme über den Zweiten Weltkrieg – Erinnerungen aber, die ich mir niemals bewusst gemacht oder niedergeschrieben hatte. Ich fand heraus, dass es den Freundinnen aus meiner Studienzeit in Berlin ebenso gegangen war, obwohl wir weder damals noch bei späteren gelegentlichen Begegnungen über unsere Erinnerungen sprachen. Wir hatten uns alle darauf konzentriert, den Krieg und die Nachkriegsjahre zu vergessen, Examina zu bestehen, Jobs zu finden, zu heiraten, Familien zu gründen ...

Die neuesten Horrorszenarien von Frauen und Kindern, die wir seit kurzem wieder vor erneuten Kriegen, erst in Syrien und sich nun über die ganze Levante und den Mittleren Osten verbreitend, fliehen sehen, brachten meine eigenen Erinnerungen lebhaft zurück und veranlassten mich, sie nieder zu schreiben. Gemeinsam mit meiner Mitherausgeberin begann ich, die Geschichten unserer Studienkolleginnen aus den späten 1950er Jahren in Berlin zu sammeln. Von denen, die im Jahr 1958 mit uns den Abschluss gemacht haben, leben nur noch neun. Solange wir noch können, möchten wir diese Erinnerungen nun zu Papier bringen.

Der Text besteht also aus 13 Berichten über die Kriegs- und Nachkriegsjahre, geschrieben von neun in Deutschland geborenen Frauen, die sich in ihrer Studienzeit in Berlin zwischen 1956 und 1958 kennen lernten, sowie einigen ihrer

Freundinnen und Ehemänner; ausser einem sind alle zwischen 1937 und 1939 geboren.

Sie erzählen von Kindheiten verbracht in Berlin und in verschiedenen Teilen des damaligen Deutschlands; von zerbombten Städten; von Angriffen durch tief fliegende Bomber direkt über ihnen; vom Zubringen endloser Nächte in überfüllten Kellern während der vielen Bombenangriffe; von der Flucht unmittelbar vor der nahenden sowjetischen Armee mit von Kanoneneinschlägen bebenden Böden unter ihren Füssen; von einer langen Flucht, die in der Nähe Dresdens endete kurz vor dem schrecklichen Bombardement und Feuersturm auf Dresden; vom knappen Verpassen des Unglücksschiffs „Gustloff", das mit vielen Flüchtlingen an Bord in der Ostsee sank; und von zwei Jahren Internierung in einem dänischen Flüchtlingslager hinter Stacheldraht nach dem Krieg.

Einige von uns waren während des Krieges in die Ostgebiete evakuiert worden, und fast alle wurden Heimatvertriebene, die nahezu ihren gesamten Besitz zurück lassen mussten, entweder gegen Ende des Krieges bei der Flucht aus den östlichen Provinzen, oder nach Kriegsende, als sie aus dem von den Russen besetzten Ostdeutschland illegal über die Grenze nach Westdeutschland gingen. Das führte dazu, dass viele in sehr engen Wohnverhältnissen landeten, meistens in Städten, in denen sie niemanden kannten und in denen es anscheinend keine Organisationen gab wie in England, die sich um die Flüchtlinge kümmerten, z.B. durch Sammeln und Verteilen von gebrauchter Kleidung, Schuhen und Haushaltsgegenständen.

Wie man den Erinnerungen entnehmen kann, erlebten manche ihre Kindheit zunächst in friedlicher Umgebung und beschreiben ein fast idyllisches Leben mit Grossfamilie, den Krieg nur aus der Ferne wahrnehmend. Aber nur zu bald rückte der Krieg immer näher, ausgebombte Städter kamen aufs Land mit Schreckensgeschichten, Nachrichten von Niederlagen an der Front sickerten zur Bevölkerung durch, ebenso Todesnachrichten von Vätern, Söhnen und Verwandten. Am Ende des Krieges und in der Nachkriegszeit waren Hunger, Angst und Unruhe unsere ständigen Begleiter, obwohl viele der Erwachsenen um uns herum ihre eigene Angst vor uns Kindern zu verbergen versuchten. Einige Berichte sind durchsetzt mit verrückten, gefährlichen Nachkriegs-Abenteuern, aber auch mit kriegsbedingten Kochrezepten und Geschichten vom Züchten von Gemüse und Blumen mitten in den Ruinen. Wir alle sind unseren Müttern für immer dankbar, dass sie so viel Kraft, Erfindungsgeist und selbstlose Fürsorge aufbrachten, um das Leben für uns bei total chaotischen Umgebungen und Bedingungen so normal wie möglich zu machen. Wir möchten dieses Buch deshalb unseren Müttern widmen.

Keiner von uns dreizehn ist professionelle/r Schriftsteller/in. Es ist auffällig – und war doch nie vorher besprochen – dass wir alle in einem völlig unemotionalen, undramatischen Stil schreiben. Das ist offenbar instinktiv der einzige Stil, der uns erlaubte, mit den Erinnerungen fertig zu werden. Und doch war es meist eine sehr emotionale Reise – einige gaben das Schreiben fast auf, überfallen von Erinnerungen, zu deren Vergessen sie so lange gebraucht hatten.

Die hier gesammelten Berichte zeigen, dass schieres Überleben, das Auftreiben von Obdach und Nahrung das Denken der Menschen im und direkt nach dem Krieg beherrschte, sowie auch eine Art von Halsstarrigkeit, weiter zu machen mit dem Leben und Verbindung zu den überlebenden

Familienmitgliedern zu halten. Auch das ist vielleicht ein Grund dafür, dass die meisten Geschichten in emotionslosem, sachlichem Stil erzählt werden.

Wir alle waren während des Zweiten Weltkriegs kleine Kinder, so dass wir natürlich nur unser eigenes Leid und unsere Ängste kannten. Als wir in den 1950ern, als Teenager, von den Verbrechen und Gräueltaten Nazi-Deutschlands, unseres Volkes, erfuhren, kamen zu den leidvollen Erfahrungen unserer Kindheit weiteres Entsetzen und Scham hinzu. Wie die meisten Deutschen liessen wir gedanklich einen eisernen Vorhang herunter, um weiter machen zu können. Einige weigern sich auch jetzt noch, ihre Erinnerungen zu befreien und zu teilen.

In den letzten Jahren sind sowohl in Deutschland als auch in Österreich etliche Zeitungsartikel, Rundfunk- und TV-Programme sowie Bücher über die Generation der WWII-Kinder, der *Kriegskinder,* erschienen. Die Journalistin und Autorin Sabine Bode hat zahlreiche Geschichten aus erster Hand aus dieser Generation zusammen getragen und schon 2004 ein zum Nachdenken anregendes Buch geschrieben, „*Die vergessene Generation: Die Kriegskinder brechen ihr Schweigen*". Einige Interviewte stellten wohl ihre Motive infrage, indem sie wissen wollten „Wollen Sie die Deutschen als Opfer darstellen?" oder „Unterstellen Sie, dass ich an einem Trauma leide?" Zu Beginn ihres Projektes stellte sie fest, dass ihre Artikel oder Scripte für TV-Programme wiederholt ignoriert und vergessen wurden, und schlussfolgerte, dass die schwer wiegende Schuld und Scham über die Verbrechen der Nazi-Aera die Erinnerungen der Kriegskinder verschüttet hatte. Inzwischen gibt es Seminare und Gesprächsrunden und nun auch Publikationen in Deutschland, und oft ist dies das erste

Mal, dass die Kriegskinder über ihre Erfahrungen sprechen – sieben Jahrzehnte nach den Ereignissen.

Die Karten, die jede der „Erinnerungen" begleiten, zeigen, dass die meisten von uns aus den nordöstlichen Teilen des damaligen Deutschlands kamen. Das liegt nahe, da wir uns in Berlin zum Studium trafen. Viele wurden in dem Teil Deutschlands geboren, der später von der russischen Armee besetzt wurde, so dass der Anteil der Flüchtlinge bzw. derjenigen, die später nach Westdeutschland entkommen wollten, aus diesen Gebieten höher ist. Der einzige Autor aus Bayern berichtet z.B. von wesentlich weniger dramatischen Kriegserlebnissen. Wenn man jedoch deutsche und österreichische Publikationen über diese Zeit betrachtet, stellt man fest, dass die Erfahrungen in beiden Ländern ähnlich sind: Sie berichten von Zerstörung, Entbehrungen und Leid, welche die schrecklichen Folgen aller Kriege sind, wie wir gerade jetzt wieder im ganzen Nahen und Mittleren Osten beobachten müssen.

Wirtschaftlicher Zusammenbruch, Diktatur, Propaganda und das durch den bewaffneten Konflikt allgegenwärtige Chaos liefern den Hintergrund für diese Berichte aus unserer Kindheit.

Ein Gedanke, der uns vereint, ist die absolute Abscheu vor Krieg und bewaffnetem Konflikt. Wir, die Autor/innen dieses Buches, schauen nicht wehmütig auf Deutschlands Vergangenheit; ganz bestimmt sehen wir uns nicht als Opfer. Im Gegenteil, wir finden es noch immer unvorstellbar und beschämend, dass die Generation unserer Eltern nichts tun konnte oder wollte, um Hitler rechtzeitig aufzuhalten, bevor die unvorstellbaren Gräueltaten an den eigenen Mitbürgern und

Menschen anderer Länder begangen wurden. Wir sind zutiefst betroffen von der Notlage der vielen Zivilisten, meist Frauen und Kinder, der jetzigen Kriege, bewaffneten Brutalitäten und Nachkriegsentbehrungen, unabhängig davon, ob sie sich auf der Gewinner- oder der Verliererseite befinden.

Barbara Ottaway, 2014

Annes Erinnerungen

Ich wurde am 25. August 1935 in Berlin-Dahlem (siehe Karte 1 für die wichtigsten im Text erwähnten Orte) geboren und habe keine Geschwister. Als die Bombenangriffe begannen, hatte meine Mutter, die überzeugt war, dass Hitler Krieg bedeutete, schon grosse Koffer gepackt mit Bettwäsche, Decken und was man schon früh einpacken konnte. Ein kleines Köfferchen mit Silber musste ich immer bei Alarm in den Keller mitnehmen. Wir hatten den Keller im Haus durch einige Stützbalken verstärken lassen. Meine Mutter hatte mein altes Gitterbett dort hingestellt, in das sie mich jedes Mal legte.

Anfang April 1943 fielen die Bomben auf unser Haus. Eine in der Nähe explodierende Mine hatte die Dachpfannen weggeblasen, so dass die Brandbomben ins Haus fallen konnten. Durch den gewaltigen Luftdruck flog ich aus dem Bett direkt in die Arme meiner Mutter, die davor stand. Der riesige Krach draussen von dem Dröhnen der Flugzeuge, dem Schiessen der Abwehrkanonen und dem säuselnden Geräusch fallender Bomben habe ich noch stets im Ohr. Die wenigen Männer, die noch da waren, auch mein Vater, liefen aus dem Keller, um festzustellen, dass das Haus schon brannte. Sie versuchten zu löschen, aber das war ein hoffnungsloses Unterfangen. Meine Mutter versuchte zu retten, was zu retten war. Da schon einige Koffer gepackt waren und wir Parterre wohnten, warf sie alles, was sie erreichen konnte, aus dem Fenster und so konnte vieles gerettet werden. All die geretteten Sachen, auch aus den vielen anderen ausgebrannten Häusern, standen tagelang auf der Strasse herum und nichts wurde gestohlen!

Ich war damals sieben Jahre alt und sass, während alle Häuser um uns herum brannten, mit unserem Mädchen in einem Gartenhäuschen gegenüber. Ich erlebte den Feuersturm, der sich nach einiger Zeit entwickelte und die Funken stieben liess. Der krachende Einsturz des Daches schliesslich hinterliess einen noch immer nicht vergessenen Eindruck.

Ich weiss nicht mehr, wie viele Tage ich noch in Berlin war nach dem Verlust unseres Hauses. Wir wohnten bei verschiedenen Bekannten, bis ein Onkel dafür sorgte, dass ich auf das Gut seines Bruders und seiner Schwester, Vetter und Cousine meiner Mutter, nach Marienmünster in Westfalen kam. Eines Tages also brachten mich meine Eltern mit Zug und Bus dorthin und fuhren dann wieder zurück nach Berlin. Der Krieg war für mich vergessen und ich genoss die Kindheit mit Kühen, Schweinen, Hühnern und vor allem mit Pferden, die meine Leidenschaft wurden. Gesund an Leib und Seele und ohne Trauma wuchs ich auf. So jedenfalls dachte ich.

Dann habe ich die folgende, kleine Erzählung gefunden, die meine Tante zu meiner Hochzeit in Form eines kleinen Lebensberichtes von mir bei ihr geschrieben hat:

'*Tief besorgt und unglücklich war Anne, wenn sie in der Schule hörte, dass ein Angriff auf Berlin gewesen war. Die Kinder brannten darauf, ihr das, was wir ihr so ängstlich verschwiegen hatten, mitzuteilen. Dass Anne Angst um ihr eigenes Leben hatte, habe ich nur bei einem schweren Gewitter erlebt, bei dem Blitz auf Blitz in den Wald fuhr und ein gewaltiger Donnerschlag dem anderen folgte, wir aber gelassen zusahen. Anne, die kleine Grossstädterin, hatte noch kein Gewitter so erlebt; sie glaubte an einen Bombenangriff, von dem wir Hinterwäldler keine Ahnung hatten und schrie:*

'In den Keller, in den Keller'. Es kostete Farbe, ihr begreiflich
zu machen, dass sie ein Naturereignis erlebte.'

Diese Erzählung zeigt, dass ich den Krieg doch nicht ganz
vergessen hatte und erklärt wohl auch die nächsten beiden
'schlummernden Erinnerungen':

Viel später, als ich verheiratet war und mein erstes Kind
erwartete, geschah folgendes: Wir wohnten in Arnhem, in
Holland, im dritten Stock eines Appartementhauses. Die
Wohnung war schön, geräumig und hatte zwei Balkons.
Sobald ich schwanger war, hatte ich jede Nacht denselben
Traum: Fliegeralarm, Gebrumm der Flugzeuge, fallende
Bomben. Ich kroch auf dem Bauch durch ein kleines Erdloch
in eine Art Bunker, voll mit Menschen – ein Klaustrophobie-
Gefühl überkam mich. Beim Wachwerden war der Traum
vorbei und vergessen. Aber in der nächsten Nacht war er
wieder da! Mit der Geburt von Andries verschwand der Traum.

Dann wurde ich wieder schwanger. Der Traum kam zurück –
jede Nacht. Warum? Da wusste ich: wahrscheinlich durch die
Verantwortung für das neue Leben fühlte ich mich in dieser
Wohnung eingeschlossen, unfrei und abhängig. Ich hatte nicht
die Möglichkeit, bei Gefahr wegzulaufen, z.B. in den Wald.
Auch gab es keinen Garten, mit dem ich uns hätte ernähren
können. Als ich im dritten Monat war, konnten wir ein Haus
'im Grünen' kaufen, mit einem Garten und ungefähr 200m
vom Wald entfernt. Sofort hörte der Traum auf.

Ich habe nie mehr vom Krieg geträumt.

Barbaras Erinnerungen

Ein Jahr vor Beginn des Zweiten Weltkrieges wurde ich in Dresden (siehe Karte 2 für die wichtigsten im Text erwähnten Orte) geboren. Vor ungefähr zwanzig Jahren sind wir zurückgegangen und fanden den Häuserblock, in denen meine Eltern damals eine Wohnung hatten, noch erhalten, umgeben von grünem Parkland. Der Häuserblock stand einmal in der Seitenstrasse einer verkehrsreichen Hauptstrasse, aber ausser diesem Block von Häusern war nach dem Bombenangriff auf Dresden nichts stehengeblieben. Ein weiterer Besuch im Jahr 2012 und Wiederaufbau hatte stattgefunden – es war sehr wenig von der grünen Parklandschaft übriggeblieben.

Meine Mutter hatte vor Bombenangriffen Angst bekommen, die grosse Städte wie Berlin, Hamburg, Leipzig und Kassel zerstört hatten. Im Herbst 1943 zog sie mit uns drei Kindern, meinen zwei jüngeren Brüdern und mir, zu ihren Eltern nach Annaberg, während mein Vater an vielen, verschiedenen Fronten kämpfte. Die Stadt Annaberg liegt im Erzgebirge, nahe der tschechischen Grenze. Meine Grosseltern hatten eine Wohnung in ihrem grossen Haus nahe am zentralen Marktplatz. Sie lag im ersten Stockwerk und hatte einen wunderbaren Kachelofen mit einer Bank, die ganz um den Ofen herum ging und auf der man sich im Winter wärmen konnte. Der Textilladen meiner Grosseltern lag im Parterre und ging bis zum Hinterhof. Wir Kinder durften nicht oft hinein, aber wenn wir hin durften, fanden wir ihn voller Ballen von wunderbarsten Stoffen, vielen verschiedenfarbigen Garnen und Knöpfen aller Formen und Farben. In dem Haus hatte jede Wohnung einen Keller, einen Teil des Dachbodens über der vierten Etage zum Wäschetrocknen und ein Plumsklo eine halbe Etage oberhalb, das mit den Bewohnern der Etage darüber geteilt wurde.

Bald nachdem wir nach Annaberg umgezogen waren, fingen die Bombenangriffe an. Ich kann immer noch keine Sirenen hören, ohne mich an diese Zeit zu erinnern. Als die Angriffe zunahmen, musste ich bei jedem Angriff meine kleinen Brüder in Eile anziehen, während meine Mutter meinen Grosseltern half. Wir mussten alle hinunter in den Keller und auf das Entwarnen durch die Sirenen warten. Meistens waren wir eine lange Zeit in diesem beengten Raum. Manchmal nahm mich mein Onkel, der im ersten Weltkrieg gekämpft hatte und ab und zu bei uns wohnte, nach oben, um die Bomber, die über uns hinwegflogen und ihre Bomben abwarfen, zu beobachten. Aber da Annaberg auf einem Berg lag, wurden die Bomben fast immer abgetrieben, ohne ihr Ziel Annaberg zu treffen, sondern sie trafen den Nachbarort Buchholz. Diese Stadt wurde fast vollständig zerstört.

Die meisten Angriffe schienen in der Nacht gewesen zu sein. Einer war jedoch an einem Nachmittag, an den ich mich erinnern kann: Unsere Mutter hatte uns in den Garten der Grosseltern, der an der Stadtmauer lag, mitgenommen. Als die Sirenen losgingen, versuchten wir nach Hause, was ungefähr eine viertel Stunde entfernt war, zurückzukommen, kamen jedoch nur bis zur Stadtmauer. Wir drückten uns gegen die Mauer, als die erste Welle Kampfflugzeuge über uns wegschoss. Als diese Welle vorüber war, schickte uns ein Mann in schwarzer Uniform, der auch dort überrascht worden war, unter die Büsche auf der anderen Seite des Weges und sagte, meine Mutter solle mein knallrotes Kleid zudecken. Meine Mutter warf ihren Mantel über mich und wir kauerten unter den Büschen und wagten keinen Blick, als die nächsten

Kampfflugzeuge über uns flogen. Sie flogen so niedrig, dass wir uns einbildeten, ihre Köpfe im Führersitz zu sehen, als wir doch mal guckten. Ich weiss nicht, ob das wahr oder eingebildet war. Nachdem die Sirenen die Entwarnung gegeben hatten, sammelten wir die leeren Patronen am Pfad auf.

Mein Vater wurde zweimal verwundet, einmal auf der Krim und das zweite Mal in Russland. Nach dem zweiten Mal wurde er zur Erholung von der Front nach Hause geschickt. Ich erinnere mich, dass es Winter war und tiefer Schnee auf allen Strassen lag. Mein Vater ging mit mir Schlittenfahren und mir wurde es wahrscheinlich zu kalt, denn ich fing an zu schreien, bis ich blau im Gesicht war. Erst war mein Vater amüsiert, dann bekam er Angst und wir kehrten schnell nach Hause zurück. Er sprach mit uns nicht viel über den Krieg – dann nicht und auch später nicht – es muss wohl zu schrecklich gewesen sein.

Das Ende des Krieges ist tief in meinem Gedächtnis verankert: vorher kamen wochenlang Ströme von Flüchtlingen durch Annaberg – Familien mit Handkarren, Kinderwagen, alles was Räder hatte, vollgepackt mit Hab und Gut und Kindern. Jetzt war der Flüchtlingsstrom mit Armeewagen durchsetzt. Dann stoppte der Strom ganz plötzlich und eine halbe Stunde lang oder so war eine unheimliche Ruhe. Plötzlich ratterte eine endlose Kette von drohend aussehenden russischen Panzern durch die Stadt, die Strasse entlang, an der das Haus meiner Grosseltern stand. Wir Kinder wollten gern die Fenster öffnen, um vielleicht eines der vielen Bonbons aufzufangen, die die russischen Soldaten den Kindern zuwarfen. Aber es wurde uns nicht erlaubt und es wurde uns gesagt, dass die Bonbons sicherlich vergiftet seien.

Chaos, Plündern, Diebstahl und Vergewaltigungen fanden statt, und meine Mutter entschied, dass wir mit meiner Tante und meinem Onkel für einige Zeit in ein benachbartes Dorf gehen sollten. So marschierten wir mit zwei Kinderwagen einige Stunden durch den Wald. Die Erwachsenen machten wahrscheinlich ein Abenteuer daraus, denn ich kann mich nicht erinnern, dass ich irgendwelche dunklen Gedanken dabei hatte.

Nach einiger Zeit kehrten wir nach Annaberg zurück. Jetzt wurde das Leben für uns alle schwerer. Es gab wenig zum Essen und jede Art von Butter, Öl oder Fett war zuende. Um Kartoffelschalen zu braten, wurde dasselbe Stück Speckschwarte immer wieder zum Einreiben der Pfanne verwendet. Meinen Grosseltern wurde das Textilgeschäft konfisziert, und im Rückblick nehme ich an, dass mein Grossvater zu dieser Zeit konfus wurde. So fiel die Aufgabe, uns alle zu versorgen und zu ernähren, an meine Mutter und Grossmutter. Sie mussten auch das Brot vor meinem Grossvater verstecken, der dabei entdeckt wurde, wie er sich manchmal mehr als seine ihm zustehende eine Scheibe Brot nahm. Zum Glück gab es Gemüse und Obst vom Garten und, für die Erwachsenen sehr wichtig: Tabak. Meine Mutter war, wie alle Frauen in dieser Zeit, sehr erfinderisch im Kochen: zum Beispiel gab es Brennnesselsuppe zum Essen und, soweit ich mich erinnern kann, beschwerten wir uns nicht. Wir sammelten auch viele Hagebutten und Holunderbeeren, die zu Saft gemacht und in Flaschen gefüllt oder zu Marmelade gekocht wurden. Bis heute kann ich nichts essen, was mit Hagebutten oder Holunderbeeren gemacht wurde, aber ohne Zweifel ist das einer der Gründe, weshalb wir alle verhältnismässig gesund aufgewachsen sind. Mein kleiner Bruder bekam Diphtherie. Er hatte sehr hohes Fieber, und schüttelte sein Peidibett und versuchte herauszuklettern, und da es keine Antibiotika gab, stand es sehr ernst um ihn.

Meine Mutter startete ein kleines Gewerbe: Sie organisierte Garn und gab es Frauen zum Stricken von Babykleidung, die sie auf dem Land gegen Butter, Mehl und alles Essbare, das sie bekommen konnte, umtauschte. Dann trug meine zierlich gebaute, kleine Mutter alles zurück auf überfüllten Zügen und 'bezahlte' damit die Frauen und das Garn und der Rest blieb für die Familie. Die meisten Erwachsenen rauchten zu dieser Zeit und wir zogen im Garten Tabak hoch. Nachdem die Tabakblätter geerntet waren, halfen wir sie auf einen Faden aufzufädeln und dann zum Trocknen auf dem Dachboden aufzuhängen. Wenn sie fertig waren, wurden sie aufgerollt und geschnitten.

'Wer ist der Mann?' fragte mein kleiner Bruder, als meine Mutter ihn in die kleine Zinkbadewanne fallen liess. Mein Vater war gerade in den Hinterhof gekommen, lange nach Ende des Krieges, wobei wir in der ganzen Zeit nichts von ihm gehört hatten und nicht wussten, ob er lebte oder gefallen war. Es war im Herbst 1946 und ich hatte meinen Vater zu dem Haus meiner Tante am Rande eines Dorfes geführt, wohin meine Mutter mit meinen beiden kleinen Brüdern gegangen war. Ich war bei meinen Grosseltern in Annaberg zurückgeblieben, da ich in die Schule musste. Mein Vater war aus einem Kriegsgefangenenlager in Polen entlassen worden, nachdem er zuvor in einem russischen Kriegsgefangenenlager gewesen war. Er hatte vorgegeben, dass seine Familie in Westdeutschland war, da er wusste, dass in der Ostdeutschen Zone, die von den Russen besetzt war, alle Männer, besonders alle Ingenieure, direkt wieder nach Sibirien abtransportiert wurden, um die Maschinen und Fabriken, die die Russen am

Ende des Krieges von Deutschland nach Sibirien gebracht hatten, wieder aufzubauen. Durch seinen Besuch in der Ostzone, um uns zu sehen, hatte er riskiert, wieder eingefangen zu werden. Deshalb dachten meine Grosseltern, dass es sicherer sei, wenn er mit mir zu meiner Tante reiste, um mit dem Rest seiner Familie zusammen zu kommen.

Nach einer kurzen Zeit ging mein Vater zurück in den 'Westen', zuerst nach Norddeutschland, um Arbeit in seinem Beruf als Bauingenieur und eine Wohnung für uns alle zu finden. Später fing er bei einer kleinen Baufirma in Schwelm, nahe bei Wuppertal in Westfalen an, einer Stadt, die kaum von Bomben zerstört worden war. Ich weiss nicht, wie er uns Bescheid gab, dass wir nun in den Westen kommen sollten. Wir mussten von Ost- nach Westdeutschland kommen, über eine Grenze, die zu dieser Zeit von russischen Soldaten bewacht wurde. Irgendwie fand meine Mutter Leute im Ort nahe der Grenze, die ihr sagten, wo man durchkommen konnte (durch den Wald) und wann es sicher war (zwischen den Kontrollen). Ich kann mich an nichts von dieser 'Wanderung' erinnern, ausser dass es ausserordentlich wichtig war, ganz still zu sein.

Im September 1947 kamen wir endlich in unsere neue Heimat: Beamte der Stadt Schwelm hatten ein Zimmer in der Wohnung eines Ehepaares für meinen Vater, seine Schwester, die inzwischen zu uns gestossen war, nachdem sie von Schlesien geflohen war, meine Mutter und uns drei Kinder zugeteilt. Man kann sich vorstellen, dass das Ehepaar nicht sehr erfreut war, uns aufnehmen zu müssen. Zum Glück hatte das Zimmer einen Balkon. Meine erfinderische Mutter startete ein Fass mit Sauerkraut, weil das die billigste Nahrung war, die man bekommen konnte. Aber die Besitzerin, die nichts im Krieg verloren hatte, beschwerte sich über den Geruch. Nach einiger Zeit fanden meine Eltern eine kleine Dachstube für meine Tante und mich und so wurde das eine Zimmer etwas weniger eng.

Ich musste in die Schwelmer Schule gehen und das war eine Qual, weil ich erbarmungslos wegen meines sächsischen Dialektes, der zugegebenerweise nicht gerade schön klingt, und wegen meiner immer selben Kleider aufgezogen wurde. Es wurde etwas erträglicher, als ich mich mit einem anderen Mädchen, Christa, anfreundete. Sie sass immer in der letzten Reihe und weinte viel. Erst viel später fand ich den Grund dafür heraus, nämlich dass sie von der französischen Zone nach Schwelm in die britische Zone gezogen waren. Zu dieser Zeit hatte jede Zone verschiedene Schulbücher und Christa hatte Angst, ihrer Mutter zu sagen, dass sie neue Schulbücher brauchte, was eine Ausgabe war, die sie sich kaum leisten konnten. Haben die Lehrer nichts gemerkt? Wir sind immer noch sehr gute Freundinnen, und sie hat mir erst vor relativ kurzer Zeit erzählt, dass sie damals Flüchtlinge waren und ganz in der Nähe von Dresden den schrecklichen Bombenangriff auf Dresden miterlebt hatten.

Meinem Vater wurde es endlich erlaubt, das obere Stockwerk eines der wenigen von Bomben getroffenen Gebäude wieder auszubauen mit dem Versprechen, dass wir diese Wohnung mieten könnten. Der Besitzer hielt jedoch sein Versprechen nicht ein und wir erhielten nur die Hälfte der Wohnung. Trotzdem waren die drei kleinen Zimmer und eine Küche eine wesentliche Verbesserung, auch wenn wir das Bad und die Toilette mit einer anderen Familie teilen mussten. Wir hatten jedoch gar keine Möbel und kein Geld, um welche zu kaufen. Was mich heute noch wundert ist, dass es keine Organisation gab, die gebrauchte Kleider, Möbel und Hausrat für Flüchtlinge sammelte, besonders für solche mit heranwachsenden Kindern.

Meine Eltern entschieden sich zu versuchen, ihre Möbel und Hausrat aus Ostdeutschland zu holen. Sie gaben uns in ein Waisenhaus in Bad Salzdetfurth bei Hannover und dachten, dass ich auf meine zwei kleinen Brüder aufpassen könnte. Sie hatten jedoch nicht mit den strengen Regeln des Waisenhauses gerechnet, die uns sofort trennten. Wir wurden durch tägliches Baden in kaltem Salzwasser sauber gehalten und die einzige Zeit, in der ich meine beiden kleinen Brüder sehen konnte, war während unserer täglichen Spaziergänge. Ich werde immer daran denken, wie wir barfuss, aber endlich alle für eine kurze Zeit zusammen spazieren gingen. Wir hatten alle drei dicke Wasserbäuche von der dünnen Suppe, die wir dort bekamen. Meine Eltern kamen endlich zurück, nachdem sie endlose Schwierigkeiten und Gefahren überlebt hatten, bei denen sie die Hälfte des Hab und Gutes als Bestechungen an Transportfirmen, Zugpersonal und russische Soldaten verloren hatten.

Langsam wurde alles besser: meine Eltern ergatterten einen Schrebergarten, wo wir Gemüse und sogar Erdbeeren anbauen konnten, und nicht jedes Paar zu klein gewordene Schuhe wurde zu einer Krise. Unser Dialekt wurde besser; wir sammelten Säcke voller Bucheckern und tauschten sie gegen Öl ein; wir schafften uns Kaninchen an, die unser Weihnachtsessen werden sollten. Aber wir Kinder erhoben Einspruch dagegen und so überlebten sie – für ein Weilchen. Dann entkam eines, oder wurde es eventuell gestohlen? Jedenfalls gab es ein bisschen später mal Fleisch zu essen! 1952 besuchte mein Bruder Christian Verwandte in Leipzig in der russischen Zone. Dort bekam er Scharlach und lag für einige Wochen in Quarantäne, bis meine Eltern endlich in der Lage waren, Penizillin hinüberzuschicken, so dass er gesund wurde und zu uns zurückkehren konnte.

In der Schule war unser Lehrplan sehr zusammengestümpert – zum Beispiel ging unser Geschichtsunterricht bis zur Napoleonischen Zeit, aber nicht weiter – es gab zu wenig Lehrer, denen man unsere Erziehung anvertrauen konnte – also gab es eine Menge aufzuholen.

Als ich 1956 nach Berlin ging um zu studieren, war die Stadt in vier Zonen, die von den vier Alliierten besetzt waren, eingeteilt. Wir hatten Kolleginnen, die in der russisch besetzten Zone lebten. Zu dieser Zeit konnten sie noch täglich herüber in das College kommen, welches in der von den westlichen Alliierten besetzten Zone lag. Eine von uns verbesserte ihre finanzielle Lage, die durch den schlechten Umtauschkurs von Ost- in Westgeld hervorgerufen war, indem sie Jenaer Glass herüber schmuggelte und es uns billiger verkaufte, als das Institut uns für im Labor zerbrochenes Glass berechnete. Wir 'Wessies' dagegen konnten es uns leisten, ab und zu nach Ostberlin ins Brecht-Theater oder sogar in die Oper zu gehen. Wie unfair war das?

In den Ferien fuhr ich mit dem Zug nach Hause zu meiner Familie, von Westberlin durch den Korridor durch die russisch besetzte Zone nach Westdeutschland. Die Züge wurden immer abgeschlossen, sodass niemand unterwegs einsteigen konnte. An der Grenze nahe Helmstedt mussten alle aussteigen und eine gründlichste Durchsuchung des Gepäcks, der Zugabteile, der Leute und ihrer Papiere wurde von DDR-Soldaten und manchmal von russischen Soldaten durchgeführt. Häufig durften einige Leute nicht wieder in den Zug einsteigen. Was war wohl ihr Schicksal?

Nach diesem finsteren Teil der Reise war es eine doppelte Freude, in Koblenz, wohin meine Familie 1956 umgezogen war, anzukommen. Manch einen Abend drehte sich unsere Unterhaltung um den Krieg – meine Brüder bereiteten sich damals auf das Abitur vor. Mein Vater war als Student in einer schlagenden Verbindung. Diese studentischen Verbindungen wurden komplett in die SA überführt. Wir konnten in unserer Naivität nicht verstehen, warum er in so einer Verbindung war und warum er an diesem Punkt nicht ausgetreten ist. So kam er als Oberleutnant in den Krieg. Wir beschuldigten und bombardierten unsere Eltern mit Fragen, warum und wie es geschehen konnte, dass Deutschland diesen schrecklichen Niedergang in Richtung Krieg und Zerstörung nehmen konnte und warum niemand in der Lage war, Hitler und die Verfolgung und Vernichtung der Juden zu stoppen. Sogar einige Jahre später, als mein Bruder in Berlin studierte, wurden diese Diskussionen während seiner Semesterferien zu Hause fortgesetzt und wurden einmal so heftig, dass er ein Jahr lang nicht nach Hause kam. Inzwischen bin ich traurig, dass wir durch diese verbalen Angriffe auf unsere Eltern den Weg verschlossen, mehr über ihre eigenen Erfahrungen während des Krieges herauszufinden. Es gab damals keine einfachen Antworten auf diese Fragen und auch heute noch gibt es für mich nicht genug Antworten, die dieses dunkle Kapitel in der Geschichte erklären könnten.

Bärbels Erinnerungen

Ich wurde im Oktober 1937 in Berlin (siehe Karte 3 für die wichtigsten im Text erwähnten Orte) als drittes Kind geboren; 1941 kam noch mein jüngster Bruder zur Welt. Zu seiner Taufe sollte die Cousine meiner Mutter aus Rio de Janeiro kommen, doch seit 1939 befand sich ja Deutschland im Krieg und so fand die Taufe ohne die Verwandten zwei Jahre später in unserer Markuskirche statt. Einen Monat danach wurde diese Kirche, die nur wenige Meter von unserem Zuhause entfernt war, durch Bomben stark beschädigt. Die Luftangriffe nahmen immer mehr zu, und wir mussten oft in den Luftschutzkeller, wo ich mich sehr fürchtete.

1943 musste meine Mutter nun mit uns vier Kindern Berlin verlassen: auf Befehl wurden kinderreiche Familien evakuiert, wir nach Bartenstein in Ostpreussen, südlich von Königsberg. Wir kamen auf einen wunderschönen Gutshof, Wiesen, Felder, Wälder, schnatternde Gänse, ausreichend Milch, Brot, Kartoffeln, herrliches, von der Gutsfrau selbst gemachtes Eis, keine Luftangriffe. Ich fühlte mich dort wohl, durfte sogar einmal in eine 'Ju2', ein (Aufklärungs-) Flugzeug, klettern, in welchem der Sohn der Gutsherrin, der leider als Jagdflieger später abgeschossen wurde, seine Mutter besuchte. Mein kleiner Bruder und ich fanden es herrlich, in der Pilotenkanzel zu sitzen, von der Dorfjugend bestaunt. Dieses Erlebnis hat wohl meine tiefe Liebe zum Fliegen geprägt. Für mich ist das Flugzeug die grösste Erfindung der Menschheit, so schrecklich auch der Einsatz als Bomber und Tiefflieger im Krieg ist.

Noch heute sehe ich mich mit der Gutsfrau am Fenster stehen, herrlich aufgeplatzte Pellkartoffeln den schnatternden Gänsen hinunter werfen. Eigentlich fürchtete ich die Gänse, wenn ich morgens an ihnen auf dem Weg zur Schule vorbei musste und sie mich laut schnatternd verfolgten.

Wir verliessen Ostpreussen nach etwa zwei Monaten und verbrachten danach in der Stadt Posen die Zeit bis zur Flucht Mitte Januar 1945. Wir wohnten dort in einem grossen Gärtnereibetrieb, den Bekannte meiner Eltern aus ihrer Studienzeit besassen. Für uns waren es Tante Lisa und Onkel Dieter mit ihren zwei, fünf und acht Jahre alten Buben. Onkel Dieter war an der Front in Narvik, in Norwegen, stationiert. So musste meine Tante den ganzen Betrieb allein verwalten.

Posen war nahe genug an Berlin, so dass mein Vater, der auch schon im ersten Weltkrieg mitgekämpft hatte, uns ab und zu besuchen konnte, bis auch er 1944 zur Wehrmacht eingezogen wurde. Er musste an verschiedenen Orten kämpfen, zum Schluss an der Ostfront in Pressburg, dem heutigen Bratislava, in der Slowakei. Eine letzte Nachricht haben wir von ihm um die Osterzeit, dem 30. März 1945, erhalten. Seit dieser Zeit gilt er als verschollen. Ich habe bis 1953, also acht Jahre lang, auf seine Rückkehr gehofft und die Radiosendungen verfolgt, wenn Listen von entlassenen Kriegsgefangenen durchgegeben wurden. Die russische Regierung behauptete dann, dass es keine Kriegsgefangenenlager mehr gäbe. All meine irrwitzigen Träume in der Nachkriegszeit, in den Schulferien nach Russland zu fahren und meinen Vater zu suchen, waren nun ausgeträumt, ich musste seinen Tod akzeptieren.

In Posen verlebte ich eine relativ unbeschwerte Zeit; keine Luftangriffe, bis auf einen mitten in der Stadt, wo der Hauptbahnhof samt unserer von meinem Vater nachgeschickten Möbel in die Luft flog. Welch eine Ironie des Schicksals!

Ich selbst genoss die Posener Zeit. Die Arbeiter nahmen mich auf dem Pferdewagen mit aufs Feld und ich plapperte ihre polnische Sprache. Ausser dem mir verhassten Hitlergruss – den rechten Arm heben und 'Heil Hitler' schreien und dies mit sechs Jahren! -, war ich in der Schule vergnügt und lernwillig.

So kam denn ganz überraschend kurz nach Weihnachten 1944 der Befehl zur Flucht. Meine Mutter war mit meinem älteren Bruder unterwegs: er war in der Nacht aus dem KVL-Lager *(Kinder-Landverschickungslager, sie waren Pflicht und es war die Vorstufe zur Hitlerjugend)* nach Hause geschickt worden. Sie kamen beide rechtzeitig zurück und los ging es, bei minus 20 Grad auf den vereisten Strassen auf offenem Pferdewagen, gezogen von unserem braven, braunen Pferd Hans und dem schwarzen Pferd Vinzenz. Wir waren sechs Kinder, von dreieinhalb bis zehn Jahren, meine Mutter, Tante Lisa sowie der polnische Kutscher, der uns wirklich sicher bis nach Bärwalde, kurz vor der Oder, brachte. Er soll, zum Glück, auch wieder nach Posen zurückgekommen sein.

Hinter uns rollten schon die russischen Panzer, ich glaubte, es sei Gewittergrollen. Die asphaltierte Hauptstrasse war unserer Wehrmacht vorbehalten, die nach Berlin rollte. Unser Treck musste die engen Waldwege über Dörfer nehmen. Ich empfand es als ein riesiges Abenteuer und wir grösseren Kinder hatten eine Aufgabe: wir liefen neben dem Fuhrwerk her und mussten Steine gegen die Hinterräder des Pferdewagens werfen, damit wir nicht in die Strassengräben rutschten. So war ich abgelenkt und habe nichts Schreckliches, was anderen passiert ist, gesehen. Dadurch haben wir auch keine Erfrierungen an den Händen und Füssen erlitten. In den Nächten fanden wir Quartier in Dörfern oder in verlassenen Bauerngehöften.

Einmal blieben wir in einer Mühle, wo uns die Müllersleute umsorgten, sie selbst wollten nicht mitfliehen.

Tante Lisa mit ihren zwei Kindern blieb in Bärwalde bei ihren Eltern, wir aber sind sofort weiter mit dem wenigen in den Händen, was jeder von uns tragen konnte. Mein kleiner Bruder zum Beispiel trug die Milchkanne. Wir erreichten den Zug, der uns über die Oder nach Berlin brachte. Wenige Stunden später wurde diese Brücke gesprengt.

Wieder in Berlin angekommen, fanden wir zum Glück unser Haus noch stehend vor. Wir fanden aber bereits zwei Ehepaare, die ausgebombt waren, darin vor und bis 1952 kamen auch noch drei Untermieter hinzu, so dass in unserer viereinhalb-Zimmerwohnung acht Leute lebten. Dort erlebten wir dann die vielen, furchtbaren Luftangriffe mit – wir waren fast vier Wochen nur im Luftschutzkeller. Draussen kamen die Tiefflieger, die uns wie Kaninchen abgeschossen hätten. Bis heute kann ich den durchdringenden Ton von Sirenen nicht ertragen und viele Jahre lang traute ich mich nicht allein in einen Kellerraum. So schön heutzutage auch ein Feuerwerk ist, beim Knall zucke ich immer noch wahnsinnig zusammen. Irgendwann tauchte ein russischer Soldat im Keller auf: Steglitz war in russischer Hand!

Die Nachkriegszeit war geprägt von Kälte, Hunger und Dunkelheit. Um uns Ruinen in denen wir herumkletterten. In einer von diesen, erst 1952 wieder aufgebaut, wohne ich jetzt wieder seit neun Jahren. Ich finde es immer wieder unfassbar, was wir damals alles erlebt haben und wie wir überhaupt überlebt haben: oft gab es kein Wasser, kein Licht, nur selten Gas für den Herd, kaum etwas zum Essen. Zuerst den Einmarsch der Russen, dann wurden wir hier im südlichen Teil

Berlins amerikanische Zone. Trotzdem war das, was wir auf die Lebensmittelkarten bekamen, weiter zum Verhungern.

Der Zusammenhalt der Erwachsenen war aber sehr freundlich; die irrwitzigsten Rezepte wurden ausgetauscht, z.B. wie man aus Kaffeesatz Kuchen, und aus Mohrrübenschalen noch Plätzchen backen kann, so sah der Alltag aus. Von den Amerikanern bekamen wir Schulspeisung und mein jüngster Bruder bekam besondere Schwedenspeisung und Lebertran.

Meine erste Schokolade bekam ich sogar von einem russischen Soldaten, der meine Mutter mit uns vier Kindern auf einem Trümmerhaufen herumklettern sah. Das löschte etwas die Angst, die wir hatten, weil kurz nach dem Krieg oft bei uns geklingelt wurde und russische Soldaten versuchten, unsere Wohnung zu durchsuchen - immer mit den gleichen Worten: 'Pistol, Pistol, Soldat, Soldat, Uri, Uri'. Das mussten auch zuerst alle Erwachsenen auf den Strassen durchmachen, meist noch dazu die Arme hoch hebend. Diese Angst sass tief, dennoch spielten wir in den Ruinen. In einem Vorgarten einer Ruine wurden Gemüse, Kartoffeln, Tomaten aber auch Blumen von meiner Mutter angepflanzt. Das Wasser schleppten wir aus dem Kanal hoch. Unser Spielzeug, unsere geliebten Teddybären, waren in Posen geblieben, aber vom Bezirksamt bekamen wir Spenden, oft aus Amerika. Lange Zeit besassen wir Würfelspiele aus Amerika und Frankreich.

Schlimm war noch einmal die Berliner Blockade 1948-1949, weil wir auch wieder zu verhungern und zu erfrieren drohten. Ich bin bis heute den vielen Piloten dankbar, die trotz hohen Risikos uns mit Essen und Kohlen versorgten und einige ihr Leben dabei lassen mussten. Unfassbar: eine Millionenstadt wie eine Burg im Mittelalter aushungern zu wollen!

Ich bin gegenüber all diesen Menschen bis heute von tiefer Dankbarkeit erfüllt, soviel Freundlichkeit wurde uns entgegengebracht, obgleich wir so vielen anderen unendliches Leid zugefügt hatten. Ich wünschte, wir würden nicht zu einer der Nationen gehören, die schon wieder am Waffenexport sehr stark beteiligt sind. Es wäre so schön, wenn es überall gelten würde: Pflugscharen statt Waffen.

Mein tiefster Dank gilt meiner Mutter, die bei all dem Wahnsinn niemals die Nerven verlor und uns beschützte und trotz allem mit viel Liebe umsorgte.

Christines Erinnerungen

Hatte sich das alles nicht zu schön angelassen damals in Ostpreussen, genauer in einem Dorf bei Insterburg, Berschkallen (siehe Karte 4 für die wichtigsten im Text erwähnten Orte), das ab 1936 den neuen echt deutschen Namen Birken tragen musste. Ein Pfarrer, eine Lehrerin, ein grosses Pfarrhaus mit grossem Garten, einen extra Gemüse- und extra Beerengarten, in den Sommermonaten betreut vom Grossvater aus Breslau, gerade aus KZ-Haft befreit und als Sozialdemokrat seines Postens als Oberstadtbaurat von Breslau enthoben, die Hauswirtschaft betreut und die dienstbaren Mädchen angeleitet von der tüchtigen Grossmutter. Dazu der Knabe (1937), 11 Monate später das Mädchen (ich 1938), Hühner, Enten, Gänse, Pfauen, die unter lautem Rufen den lieben langen Tag ihr Rad schlugen, bunte Schweine....., nahe am Wald mit Elchen, „die in die Ewigkeit lauschten", mit Wolfsgeheul in den langen Winternächten.

Die ersten Jahre - und ab 1941 belebte noch ein Schwesterchen die Szene mit - erinnere ich aus unerschütterlicher Geborgenheit heraus als rührig, einfallsreich, lustvoll verschwörerisch ... nicht zu aller Freude ... nach dem Froschkönig im tiefen Brunnen fahnden, die armen Schweinchen aufs Feld in die Freiheit entlassen, bei grosser Hitze den Bienlein Wasser zum Trinken in den Bienenstock leeren, mit der Minisäge aus der Sonntagswundertüte sich daran machen, meterdicke Bäume umzulegen und immer so fort.... unbeschwert „wie Schmetterlinge durch Wiesen und Felder gaukelnd," so die Fama.

Schon 1939 wurde unser Vater als vorgeschobener Beobachter und Feldprediger eingezogen. Von da an lastete die gesamte

Gemeindearbeit auf den Schultern unserer noch nicht 30jährigen Mutter. Sie fühlte es als ihre Aufgabe, die weitläufige, grosse Gemeinde in (kirchen-) politisch schwerer Zeit zusammenzuhalten. Man suchte Trost und Hilfe bei ihr, (deren Herz selbst so schwer war) wenn Ehepartner, Söhne, Väter im Krieg gefallen waren, während sie immer noch Ariernachweise erstellen musste. Wie manchen sie „richtig" gefärbt hat, hat sie mit sich genommen.

Von all der herrschenden Not waren wir Kinder in unserer Idylle ferngehalten. Was sich drastisch ändern sollte, als ich allein auf freiem Feld von einem Tiefflieger mit ohrenbetäubendem Getöse überflogen wurde. Noch nie hatte ich einen Flieger gesehen. Erstmals FÜHLTE ich, DAS WAR WAS MIT KRIEG, und dass mein Vater in grosser Gefahr sein musste. (Da hatte er Stalingrad – ohne dass wir Kinder davon gewusst hätten - gerade überlebt). Ich war aufgerüttelt, begann bang bedrückte, sorgenvolle Gesichter bei den Erwachsenen wahr zu nehmen. Davon beunruhigt und verängstigt, sprang ich - auf Hilfe sinnend - mit einem Satz von der hoch fliegenden Schaukel, und forderte auf unser Haus blickend Gott heraus: „Bring mir meinen Vater heil aus dem Krieg zurück, sonst werde ich nie mehr an Dich glauben." Da war ich um die vier.

Zu der Zeit in etwa weilte ich bei einem Königsberger Onkel, bei dessen Heimkehr aus seiner Kanzlei ich ihn freudig mit „Heil Hitler" begrüsste. Der sonst so Gütige versetzte mir eine nachhaltige Ohrfeige. Als er später die Verteidigung von Ostpreussens Gauleiter Koch ablehnte, verschwand er im KZ für immer.

Im Frühherbst 1943 kamen meine Schwester und ich zu den Breslauer Grosseltern, wohl um unsere Mutter zu entlasten. Gottesdienste, Taufen, Beerdigungen übernahm zwar der Königsberger Grossvater, aber die menschlich immer desolater werdende Gemeindearbeit hing allein an der Mutter. Zu meinem grossen Unglück blieb mein Bruder in Birken zurück, da er eingeschult wurde. Unsere erste Trennung. Ein erstes Erdbeben.

Die Grosseltern waren von Breslau in eine Mietwohnung nach Bad Obernigk umgezogen. Wir waren lieb betreut. Naturschwimmbad im Sommer, Zoobesuche und die Kurkonzerte am Sonntag waren unsere kleine Welt. Und trotzdem: Es quälte mich eine bohrende Sehnsucht nach der Mutter und dem Bruder, eine Einsamkeit, die ich niemandem anvertrauen konnte. (Jahrzehnte später las ich im Tagebuch meiner Mutter aus jener Zeit, wie unendlich sie unter der „Zerrissenheit der Familie" gelitten hat). Wie häufig wir in jener Zeit in grosser Hast in den Luftschutzkeller eilten, erinnere ich mich nicht mehr, nur dass wir es mussten und an die Dunkelheit und das grosse Schweigen. Allabendlich wurden die Verdunkelungsrouleaux herabgezogen, „um den Feind auszusperren". Wie naiv waren wir, bis wir auf die Idee kamen, seitlich zum Schlitz hinaus zu spähen ... und sahen abgeworfene „Christbäume", die die Nacht lautlos gespenstisch erhellten. (Bis heute mag ich kein Feuerwerk, wie schön diese leuchtenden Gebilde auch sein mögen). Das Nahrungsangebot wurde einseitig, denn in Obernigk hatten wir keinen Garten. Auf den Tisch kamen Mehlsuppe, Kartoffeln, Mohrrüben, Sauerkraut, manchmal Quark, mit Rüben verlängerte Marmelade zum Frühstücksbrötchen. Aber Hunger war uns noch fremd.

Im August 1944 wurde ich 3 Monate vor meinem 6. Geburtstag eingeschult. Mein Schulranzen: eine ausgediente Aktentasche meines Grossvaters, über die ich todunglücklich war angesichts der „richtigen" Ranzen meiner Mitschüler. Aber die Schiefertafel und die kleine Fibel (das erste Lesebuch) in der grossen Mappe, die waren mein heissgeliebter Besitz.

Im Spätherbst 1944 kam unsere Mutter mit dem Bruder aus Ostpreussen nach Obernigk. Die Stimmung war, als ob etwas ganz Schlimmes passiert sein musste. Wir erfuhren, dass unsere Tante, Omas jüngste Tochter, Mutters Schwester, mit ihrem Neugeborenen Büblein im Kindbett gestorben war. Zurück blieb das noch nicht einjährige Herrmännchen. Er wurde unser kleiner nicht mehr aus unserem Leben wegzudenkender Bruder.

Sein zu Hause war in Sorau in der Oberlausitz, wohin Mutter Schwesterchen Renate brachte, und die beiden Kleinen von einer fernen Tante betreuen liess, während sie mit Grossvater zurück nach Ostpreussen ging, wo sie im Pfarrhaus 19 Frauen und Kinder aufgenommen hatte, die vor den Angriffen auf Königsberg geflohen waren. Erst mussten sie alle an einen sicheren Ort zur Weiterreise in den Westen gebracht werden. Unsere Familie verstreut auf Ostpreussen, Lausitz, Schlesien. Und der Vater wo?

Wohl um die Zeit, als Mutter und Grossvater in jenem eisigen Winter sich selbst auf die Flucht aus Ostpreussen und über weite Strecken zu Fuss durch die Wälder begaben, bekamen wir in Obernik Räumungsbefehl. Das hiess, sich am nächsten Morgen am Bahnhof einzufinden, um mit einem der Pferdewagen, Schlitten, wegtransportiert zu werden. Als wir eintrafen, waren alle Schlitten schon überfüllt. Das sollte unser

Glück sein. Später erfuhren wir, dass alle Schlitten umgekippt waren. Viele Menschen wurden schwer verletzt oder verloren ihr Leben.

Nach einem quälenden Tag der Ungewissheit, den wir auf dem bitterkalten Bahnhof verbrachten, fuhr gegen Abend ein Zug ein, der von der Menge Wartender im Nu gestürmt war. Zerborstene Fensterscheiben, eingefrorene Toiletten, Temperaturen um die 25 Minusgrade. Oma wickelte meinen Bruder und mich in Grossvaters Wolfspelz, sozusagen alles, was sie mitgenommen hatte. Auch meine Schildkrötpuppe und die Fibel mussten zurückbleiben. Oft hielt der Zug nachts verdunkelt auf freiem Feld, um nicht ins Visier feindlicher Fliegergeschwader zu geraten. Nie konnte man wissen, wann es weiter gehen würde. Trotzdem hielt Oma uns zur Waggontür raus, weil wir mal „mussten". Als wir zurück kamen, war Opas Wolfspelz gestohlen. Die Schreie verzweifelter Mütter, deren Kinder erfroren waren oder starben, weil sie krank waren, erfüllten den Waggon.

In Sorau fanden wir nach langen Irrfahrten wieder zusammen. Kurz darauf kam auch hier der Räumungsbefehl. Unser Tross von sieben Personen sollte nach Meissen, wo unser Vater für uns bei zwei Pfarrfamilien Unterschlupf finden konnte. Die Bahnsteige waren überfüllt von Menschen und Gepäck, dass kein Fuss mehr zu setzen war. Ein einfahrender Zug zerfetzte Federbetten. In dem dichten Gewölk von „Frau Holle", das in Augen, Nase und Mund drang, erkämpfte sich die Masse tumultartig Zutritt zu den Wagen. So viel Schreie wie Federn in der Luft, und die verzweifelte Angst, in dem Getöse allein zurückzubleiben und seine Lieben zu verlieren.

Dann begann für uns Meissen. Auf irgendwelchen Gleisen ausserhalb des Bahnhofs machte unsere Mutter unter Zügen voller Militär den aus, in dem unser Vater stand, in einem Viehwagen an der Absperrstange. Ein paar Worte noch, dann setzte der Zug sich in Bewegung. Ich weinte und winkte Vati Aufwiedersehn. Zum letzten Mal.

Das Haus von Pfarrer P., in dem wir zwei immer dunkle Zimmer zugewiesen bekamen, stand an der Uferstrasse an der Elbe, wenige Schritte von der Elbbrücke entfernt. Die Grosseltern suchten allabendlich ihre Schlafstatt einige Fussminuten entfernt bei Pfarrer S. auf. Der Weg führte eine Steinmauer entlang, die von der anderen Elbuferseite abends häufig unter Beschuss stand. Wenn man bei den Grosseltern schlafen sollte, musste man diese Mauer Mutterseelen allein passieren. Irgendwann wurde dieser Horrortrip eingestellt.

Auf dem Klo stibitzte ich zwei fein zurechtgeschnittene Zeitungsklopapierchen und riss mir daraus zwei Püppchen, die ich miteinander spielen lassen konnte. Als das Entwenden der kostbaren Papierchen entdeckt wurde, führte es zum mittleren Desaster.

Bald häuften sich vermehrt die Fliegeralarme, es folgte die gehetzte Flucht in den Luftschutzkeller. Grossvater trichterte uns ein, alles Notwendige im Dunkeln sofort greifen können zu müssen, auch für die Kleinen, die nicht wach werden wollten. Im Keller verfolgten wir das ferne Grummeln, das immer breiter ausfächernde Näherkommen und unter Kopfeinziehen des Überfliegens, endlich das Entfernen der Fluggeschwader. Vorbei. Entwarnung. So auch in jener Nacht, als Abertausende in Dresden und die Flüchtlinge auf den Elbwiesen den Tod fanden. Wir krochen aus dem Keller in den Hof und sahen über dem fernen Dresden den Himmel glutrot brennen.

In den Tagen danach geschah Unvorstellbares. Kolonnen von Pferdefuhrwerken mit Dunklem beladen überquerten die Elbbrücke. Es dauerte, bis die Kinderaugen das Unfassbare realisierten. Die Ladung, das waren verkohlte menschliche Körper.

Munchs Gemälde „Der Schrei" kannte ich noch nicht, aber damit könnte ich das helle Entsetzen von damals beschreiben.

Mutter wollte mich ablenken und organisierte Turnunterricht für mich. Dort traf ich verspätet ein und sah in der Garderobe lauter leere Kleider hängen. Ich flüchtete in Panik und ging nie mehr dort hin, auch nicht mehr in die Schwimmstunde, weil das weite Hallenbad mir Angst machte. Die Elbbrücke wurde noch gesprengt (herumfliegende Dachziegeln verschütteten das erste zarte Grün von Opas ausgesäten Möhren), bevor am achten Mai Waffenstillstand ausgerufen wurde. Das hiess, Ende der Beherbergung in den „gastlichen" Pfarrhäusern, wo wir uns von Wassermaissuppe und Wassermaisbrei „ernährt" hatten, während ihre Vorratskeller satt gefüllt waren.

Mutter hatte nahe Dresden eine Gemüse- und Obstgärtnerei ausfindig gemacht. Frau Friedel, deren Mann noch nicht zurückgekehrt war, brauchte dringend Erntehilfe. Mit einem sogenannten Panjewagen (einem leichten Bauernwagen, eigentlich von einem Pferd gezogen) und einem hochrädrigen Puppenwagen, beladen mit wieder eigenem Geschirr, für dessen Unversehrtheit ich die Verantwortung trug, pilgerten wir an einem heissen Maitag den langen Weg von Meissen nach Coswig. Wir bekamen einen herzlichen Empfang mit einem reich gedeckten Tisch, wie wir seit Monaten nicht gesehen hatten. Tante Friedel und Mutter ernteten, wir halfen mit, Grossmutter schwang das Zepter in der Küche, Grossvater gab uns und Friedels Kindern Schulunterricht. Wir lebten im Paradies. Einzig die lange Hungerzeit machte sich bemerkbar. Ich bekam Furunkel entlang der Wirbelsäule und der Schienenbeine. Es begann eine endlos lange Tortur des Verbändewechselns. Friedels Mann kam zurück. Die beiden Frauen sollte eine lebenslange Freundschaft verbinden. Doch die Zeit der Ernte und damit sich nützlich machen zu können, war vorbei.

In Halle an der Saale hatte Omi aus Königsberg, deren Schwiegersohn gebürtiger Hallenser war, bei einem Pfarrer unterkommen können. Diesem war die Betreuung einer grossen Wohnung eines Theologieprofessors, der in den Westen geflohen war, anvertraut worden. Unsere Grossfamilie kam ihm gelegen, damit die Wohnung nicht ganz von Russen belegt würde. Aber zwei waren da, sie trommelten nachts an unsere Schlafzimmertür und schrien „Frau, Frau". Furchtbar für unsere Mutter, aber auch für uns. Mutter sass absprungbereit auf dem Fensterbrett. Nach unten ging es tief. Die Kerle wurden ausgewechselt gegen einen gebildeten Major, bei dem wir Kinderfunk hören durften. Beissende Stiche bekamen wir über die Nächte: Wanzen! Kammerjäger, versiegelte Zimmer, wieder Durcheinander....

Der Hunger in Halle! Omas „Sparkloss" aus reinen Kartoffelschalen mit Majoran gewürzter Mehlsauce war ein Festessen. Einmal, die Speisekammer war endgültig leer, fand ich eine Tüte mit weissem Pulver auf einer Mauer. Oma probierte erst selbst auf Geniessbar. Dann schliefen wir mit wohligen Mehlsuppenbäuchen ein. Als mir an einem

Monatsanfang die gesamten Lebensmittelkarten gestohlen wurden, spendeten mir alle 30 Mitschülerinnen ihr Schulspeisepausenbrötchen. Eine unglaubliche Solidarität. Manche hätten ihr Brötchen selbst gebraucht. Wir lebten jeder von vier trockenen Brötchen pro Tag. Opa kam ins Spital mit Krebsverdacht, aber seine furchtbaren Schmerzen waren die Därme, die sich aneinander rieben. Ich wurde landverschickt. Ein Bus lud mich und die anderen Kinder im Dorf Kossebau bei Stendal im Wirtshaus ab. Alle hatten sofort ihre Gastfamilie. Ich blieb an jenem Mittag allein zurück, bis am Abend sich noch ein Bauer meiner erbarmte. Als erstes stellte er mich auf die Waage: Mit fast 9 Jahren knapp 18 Kilo.

Bauer B. war ein Glück für uns. Er liess Mutter kommen, und wir konnten auf seinen Feldern Ähren lesen. Ein Jahr zuvor war es irgendwo ein Kampf vieler um jede Ähre und die Nächte auf drei Wirtshausstühlen. Auf dem Küchentisch wurde Korn um Korn entspelzt, dann das kostbare Gut per Kaffeemühle gemahlen. Ich erinnere Dauerblasen in der Handfläche.

Grossvater bekam in Halle einen Schrebergarten zugeteilt. Das war ein Flugfeld; Opa, der Bruder und ich mussten Pflasterstein um Pflasterstein ausgraben und wegkarren, um an etwas Erdsubstanz zu kommen. Opa machte daraus einen Wundergarten mit Kartoffeln, Gemüse und Tabak. Oma quetschte aus (wie auch gesammelten?) Zuckerrüben mit Hilfe unserer Kindergewichte auf einer Presse Zuckerrübensirup. Zu Weihnachten gab es aus UNSEREM MEHL und UNSEREM ZUCKERRÜBENSIRUP ein grosses Pfefferkuchenhaus. Mutter lud zu unserem Entsetzen eine „Hundertschaft" Kinder unter Zeitungsgirlandendekoration zum Essfest ein, weil es anderen Kindern schlechter gehe als uns.

Wir Kinder spielten in jener Zeit „hauptamtlich" Theater: Eigenes Drehbuch, eigene Bühnenausstattung. Mitdarsteller Nachbar- und Russenkinder. In Mutters Tagebuch liest sich das so: „Die Kinder sind alt und altklug geworden und spielen nur Krieg".

Halle nahm (wohl im März) 1949 ein jähes Ende, als eine Russin Mutter warnte, dass die kommunistische Partei es auf unseren Bruder zwecks „Förderung" in Richtung Moskau abgesehen hatte. Mutter nahm beide Knaben, um via Berlin mit Kohleflugzeug mit ihnen zu fliehen. „Was flennst", fragte einer am überfüllten Flughafen sie, die so viel Geld für den Flug nicht hatte. Sie soll warten. Er brachte Tickets, die er anderen fürs Doppelte verkauft hatte. So viel gerissene Empathie gab's damals. Grossvater und eine Freundin von Mutter begleiteten Schwester und mich an einen Grenzort, auf dass wir die grüne Grenze überqueren würden. Wohin? Wir wurden abgefangen, auch eingelocht, und zurück geschickt. Grossvater, der nicht in den Westen wollte, entschied nach vielen missglückten Versuchen, dass wir zu viert mit Oma in den Westen flüchten. In einer dunklen Spelunke erwartete uns des Nachts eine Frau, die uns durch eine verminte Kohlengrube führen sollte. Geräuschlos. Schwester brachte ich einzig zum Schweigen, dass wir alle sterben würden, wenn sie weiter plärre (dabei heulte ich zuinnerst selbst, denn die Grosseltern waren weit voraus). Der Rest ist blackout. Ich kam erst wieder zu mir in einem Weiss bezogenen Bett, jemand zog weisse Vorhänge auf, liess die Sonne herein und rief „ach Gottchen, die armen Kinder".

Eine erneute Zerrissenheit der Familie nahm mit diesem Frühjahr 1949 ihren Anfang. Die Grosseltern bei ihrem Sohn in Hamburg, Herrmännchen, dessen Vater sich seiner erinnerte, in einem Waisenhaus in Bielefeld, wo ihm die „gütigen" Schwestern noch sein einziges, sein Bärchen wegnahmen. Das Kerlchen war haltlos verloren. Unsere Mutter in einer Dachkammer mit dem Bruder in Wuppertal bei einer Kriegerwitwe aus dem ersten Weltkrieg, deren Sohn unser Vater bei Stalingrad begraben musste. Schwester Renate und ich fanden uns in einem Waisenhaus in Schwelm wieder. In einen Saal von um die 25 Mädchen stellte man uns ein gemeinsames Bett mit einer schweren Militärzudecke.

Sonntags besuchte Mutti uns, und dann immer die Abschiede bis zum nächsten Sonntag.... Wie lange ging das? Hab es nie erfragt, wie so vieles. Die Wende kam, als der Bruder unseres Vaters, Kinderarzt, uns bei sich aufnahm in Mettmann, unweit Wuppertals. Das fühlte sich an wie Familie: Papa, Mama, Kinder. Onkel liess mich die Prüfung fürs Gymnasium machen, und jeden Morgen lief ich singend vor Glück in die Schule. Das Glück war von kurzer Dauer. Wir mussten zurück ins Waisenhaus. Dort war man als Gymnasiastin aussätzig, im Gymnasium war man als aus dem Waisenhaus kommend aussätzig. Die morgendliche Wassergriessmilchsuppe kam mir zurück. Ohne Essen ging ich zur Schule. Ich wurde in die letzte Bank gesetzt, weinte offenbar ständig, hatte die falschen Schulbücher und wurde für dumm gehalten. Mutter konnte ich keine neuen Schulbücher zumuten. Die Mutter einer Klassenkameradin Barbara schlug ihrer Tochter vor, mich einmal zu ihnen nach Hause zu bringen. Das war ein unendliches Glücksgefühl, weg von der Waisenhausatmosphäre, Mutter, Vater, Kinder. Daraus wurde eine lebenslange Freundschaft, ja Geschwisterschaft.

Dank - muss man später sagen - einer unerklärbaren Fiebererkrankung von mir suchte der Heimkinderarzt für uns eine Wohnung in Wuppertal. Zwei Zimmer, Küche und Plumpsklo auf halber Etage zu teilen mit einer weiteren Familie. Keine Fenster gab es da noch. Wenn Gewitter sich mächtig übers Haus hermachten, dann ojeh. Nach oben ins Dach gab es noch keine Decke, alles offen. Wir hatten, das war unser Mobiliar, einen Eisenofen in Grösse eines Hockers zum Sitzen oder um unreife Birnen – die dazumalige einzige Nahrung - zu kochen und EIN Bett für VIER Personen mit einem tiefen Loch in der Matratze, das wir mit den wenigen nicht gerade zum Gebrauch benötigten Kleidern füllten. Mutti las uns jeden Abend im gemeinsamen Bett Geschichten vor. Wir lebten trotzdem im Gefühl allen Glücks auf Erden.

So ganz war das nicht. Unsere in Hamburg nicht glücklichen Grosseltern zogen zu uns in die Miniwohnung, aber sie halfen uns sehr. Wir brachten uns mit Heimarbeit über die Runden, stundenlang auch Kinderarbeit, ein Beitrag zum gemeinsamen Überleben, nie beklagt, während andere Kinder draussen spielten. Kam mal ein Pfarrer vorbei und fand es so schön, die Familie so traulich vereint am Heimarbeitstisch. „Hausarbeit ist Lausarbeit", schrie ihn meine Schwester an. Der kam nie wieder. Den Gottesknaben hat es nie interessiert, dass mein Bruder und ich uns in ein Paar Schuhe teilen mussten, der eine zum Glück zur Schule am Vormittag, der andere nachmittags, aber um alles auf der Welt musste man rechtzeitig zur Übergabe sein.

Im Sommer 1950 wurden wir Kinder zu verschiedenen entfernt Verwandten für drei Monate in die Schweiz eingeladen. Das war Paradies und Schlaraffenland in einem. Wir durften wieder Kinder sein! Es gab keine Trümmergrundstücke... Die Verwandten waren uns herzlich zugetan, fröhlich, unkompliziert. Ich bekam das erste Paar Schuhe seit Jahren, das mir passte (Marke Bally), Tante schleppte Bücher über Bücher an, eine Früchteschale wurde jeden Morgen frisch gefüllt, es gab Fleisch zu Mittag und am Samstag eine grosse Badewanne mit eigenem Wasser in der Waschküche. Ich erbte die wunderschönen Kleider meiner gleichaltrigen „grossen Schwester". Ab da wurde ich nicht mehr wegen meiner immer gleichen ärmlichen Kleider in der Schule verlacht.

Wenig danach geschah, dass Adenauer Kriegsgefangene aus Russland frei bekam. Im Radio kamen die Namen. Es war wie allen Lebens leerberaubt, wenn wieder das S... (der Anfangsbuchstabe des Familiennamens) vorüberging.

Opa kämpfte Jahre um seine durch Nazideutschland verlorene Rente. Er bekam eine Abfindung nur unter der Prämisse zu unterschreiben, dass er Namen weder wer ihn ins KZ gebracht hatte, noch seine dortigen Peiniger je preis geben werde. Erst 1952 begann für uns in einer geräumigeren Wohnung mit Bad ein einigermassen „normales" Leben. Mutter bekam wieder eine Stelle als Teilzeitlehrerin in meiner Schwelmer Schule. Der Direktor dort brachte sie noch um ihre Altersversorgung.

Trotz allem unheilvoll Erlebtem, und dem, was hier gar nicht zur Sprache kommen sollte, empfinde ich Dankbarkeit dafür, dass wir immer noch so gnädig durch diese schweren Zeiten kommen durften. Da spreche ich bestimmt für unsere tapfere starke Mutter mit.

Dörthes Erinnerungen

Am Sonntag, dem 27. August 1939, wurde ich als viertes Kind meiner Eltern in Meuselwitz (siehe Karte 5 für die wichtigsten im Text erwähnten Orte) bei Altenburg in Thüringen geboren. Ich bin ein Sonntagskind und ein Friedenskind – gerade noch.

Am ersten September 1939 fielen die deutschen Truppen in Polen ein und damit begann der Zweite Weltkrieg. Meine Mutter erzählte immer, dass schon eine Woche vorher Lebensmittelkarten an die Bevölkerung ausgegeben wurden. Also war man eigentlich auf kommende Ereignisse vorbereitet und ich frage mich, wie bange es meiner Mutter wohl war, dass ihr viertes Kind in diese Zeit hineingeboren wurde? Für die Propaganda war es der Überfall Polens auf Deutschland und 'seit heute früh um 4.45 Uhr wird zurück geschossen' - heute wissen wir es besser. Meine Mutter lag noch im Wochenbett, ich war, wie alle Kinder zu der Zeit eine Hausgeburt und die Hebamme des Ortes kam jeden Tag. Was haben die Frauen wohl miteinander gesprochen?

Mein ältester Bruder wurde 1933, meine Schwester 1935 und mein zweiter Bruder 1937 geboren. Anfang 1939 war meine Familie nach Meuselwitz gezogen, und war neu dort. Fühlte meine Mutter sich allein? Mein Vater wurde 1940 als Soldat eingezogen, da war meine Mutter mit dem fünften Kind schwanger. Mein dritter Bruder wurde dann im November 1940 geboren. Wie erging es ihr da? Und wie schaffte sie alles mit den kleinen Kindern?

Mein Vater hatte „Glück", denn er kämpfte mit den Truppen der Wehrmacht in Norwegen und wurde wohl von den schlimmsten Kriegsgräueln verschont. Aber darüber wissen wir eigentlich auch nichts, denn er erzählte, wie viele Väter, nach dem Krieg nichts. Mein jüngster Bruder und ich kannten unseren Vater nur von kurzen Heimaturlauben und erkannten ihn, als er 1947 aus der Kriegsgefangenschaft zurück kam, nicht wieder.

Unsere Mutter musste dann die fünf Kinder alleine durch den Krieg bringen. Zunächst schien der Krieg noch fern von uns stattzufinden. Allerdings kamen evakuierte Familien aus dem heftig bombardierten Ruhrgebiet und dem Saarland zu uns und wir rückten zusammen, um zwei Familien bei uns aufnehmen zu können. Mit dem Nachbarhaus teilten wir uns einen Garten und es waren immer viele Erwachsene und Kinder da, was sehr schön war. An meine frühe Kindheit erinnere ich mich nur in einem Radius vom Haus, durch den Garten bis zum Gartentor. Weiter traute ich mich nicht, meine Geschwister waren da schon etwas abenteuerlustiger. Es hiess, ich sei ein ängstliches Kind gewesen, aber das ist mir vielleicht mit der Muttermilch eingegeben worden?

Unsere Stadt blieb bis zum November 1944 von Bombenangriffen verschont, dann fand der erste verheerende Bombenangriff statt. Trotzdem heulten auch schon vorher die Sirenen, wenn die Bombengeschwader über uns hinweg flogen Richtung Leipzig. Wenn die Sirenen heulten, mussten wir - meistens nachts - in den Luftschutzkeller des Nachbarhauses, denn unser Keller bestand nur aus einem kleinen Raum. Meine ältere Schwester musste jedes Mal vor Angst und Aufregung auf 'den Topf', was immer eine Geduldsprobe für meine Mutter war. Noch heute erinnern mich heulende Sirenen an die Bombenangriffe.

Der letzte schwere angloamerikanische Luftangriff war am 20.2.1945. Unsere Stadt wurde zu 80% zerstört. Sehr viele Tote (das jüngste Opfer war vier Wochen alt), Schwerverletzte und Obdachlose waren die Bilanz dieses Krieges. Die Bomben sollten die Munitionsfabrik mit umfangreichen Rüstungsprodukten - dort wurden Panzerfäuste hergestellt - in der Nähe treffen, was auch zu 80% gelang, doch leider sind auch viele Bomben zu früh abgeworfen worden und haben viele Häuser in der Stadt und das benachbarte Rittergut völlig zerstört. Nach der Entwarnung sahen wir, wie es lichterloh brannte und viele Vögel in den Flammen umkamen. Unser Haus hatte kein Dach mehr, Türen und Fenster waren herausgeflogen. Dieser Anblick war für mich ein grosser Schock und dieses Trauma verfolgt mich noch heute manchmal. Als meine Mutter sah, wie erschüttert ich war, versuchte sie mich zu trösten und sagte, dass wir sehr glücklich sein könnten, dass wir alle überlebt hatten und unverletzt waren. Ja, wir haben den schweren Angriff überlebt im Gegensatz zu vielen, vielen anderen. Diese schlimme Nacht verbrachte unsere Familie in zwei verschiedenen Kellern. Mein ältester Bruder hatte Scharlach mit sehr hohem Fieber, so dass meine Mutter gemeinsam mit ihm in dem kleinen Keller unseres Hauses zugebracht hat. Wir anderen waren im Nachbarhaus. Man kann sich vorstellen, wie gross die Freude war, dass wir alle unverletzt wieder zusammen waren. Mein Bruder kam noch am gleichen Tag mit dem ersten Krankentransport in das Krankenhaus der benachbarten grösseren Stadt, wo er sechs Wochen bleiben musste.

Rings um unser Haus war viel Schutt. Ich erinnere mich, dass mein jüngerer Bruder und ich geholfen haben, die Trümmer in kleinen Eimern an die Strasse zu tragen. Alle Produktionsbetriebe standen still, Gas- und Wasserleitungen waren zerstört. Viele Männer waren im Krieg umgekommen oder in Kriegsgefangenschaft. Die Stadt musste viele Evakuierte und Umsiedler aufnehmen und hatte Verantwortung gegenüber den ausgehungerten Kriegsgefangenen und Zwangsarbeitern in den Lagern. In der zerstörten Munitionsfabrik waren neben Fremdarbeitern aus ganz Europa auch Häftlinge aus den Konzentrationslagern Buchenwald und Auschwitz inhaftiert. Das wussten viele der Einwohner zur damaligen Zeit nicht. Ich erinnere mich nur, dass von Fremdarbeitern gesprochen wurde. Das ganze Ausmass des Grauens dieses Krieges wurde vielen erst danach bekannt.

Es war nach diesem Bombenangriff eine chaotische Situation entstanden. Es herrschte eine grosse Lebensmittelknappheit und es war sehr schwer für unsere Mutter, uns fünf Kinder und sich selbst zu ernähren. So tauschte sie bei den Bauern Silberbestecke, Wertgegenstände und Kleidung gegen Brot, Kartoffeln und Mehl. Viele Bauern haben diese Notsituation sehr ausgenutzt und ich habe meine Mutter oft traurig erlebt.

Mit der Befreiung durch die Amerikaner im April 1945 gingen der Krieg und zwölf Jahre Naziherrschaft in unserer kleinen Stadt zu Ende. Kinder suchten den Kontakt zu den amerikanischen Soldaten, so auch mein zwölfjähriger Bruder, der schon in der Schule etwas Englisch gelernt hatte und sich notdürftig verständigen konnte. Er tauschte Briefmarken mit einem amerikanischen Soldaten, der dann auch bald unserer Mutter seine Wäsche zum Waschen und Bügeln brachte. Das bescherte uns dann Kernseife und Lebensmittel, worüber wir überglücklich waren. Doch bald zogen die Amerikaner ab und so leider auch unser befreundeter amerikanischer Soldat. Mein Bruder hatte noch lange Kontakt zu ihm und seiner Familie, durch die wir dann in den 50iger Jahren noch regelmässig 'Care-Pakete' geschickt bekamen. Auch das eine sehr willkommene Unterstützung.

Laut Abkommen der Alliierten in Jalta kam es zum Gebietsaustausch und die Amerikaner zogen ab und die Sowjetarmee marschierte ein und besetzte unsere Stadt. Ich habe oft für meine Mutter eingekauft und wurde einmal auf dem Heimweg von unendlich vielen Panzern, die die Hauptstrasse entlang donnerten, überrascht. Ich blieb am Rande der Strasse stehen - mit vielen anderen - und schaute diesem Einmarsch der Russen zu. Ganz besorgt stand plötzlich meine Mutter vor mir, die sich schon grosse Sorgen über mein langes Fortbleiben gemacht hatte. Mit meinen knapp sechs Jahren bekam ich mit, dass die Erwachsenen mit grossen Ängsten den Russen entgegensahen. Nach der Freude vieler, dass uns die Amerikaner befreit hatten, kam nun die Angst vieler, was nun geschehen würde. Schliesslich hatte die Nazi-Propaganda die Russen als Kommunisten im schrecklichsten Licht gemalt (und wie man später hörte, hat die Bevölkerung besonders unter den Plünderungen und Vergewaltigungen der ersten einmarschierenden Sowjet-Truppen gelitten.)

Jetzt begann die schlimme Nach-Kriegszeit mit Hunger und der Beseitigung der Trümmer. Wir gingen oft mit unserer Mutter zum Ährenlesen und 'stoppeln' über die von den Bauern abgeernteten und dann freigegebenen Felder. Ich erinnere mich, dass mein ältester Bruder einmal die von ihm 'gestoppelten' Kartoffeln zu Hause gekocht und ganz allein gegessen hatte. Die Jungen hatten immer grossen Hunger.

1947 kam dann endlich mein Vater aus französischer Gefangenschaft zurück. Er hatte sich erst zu seiner Mutter und zwei Schwestern in die britische Zone entlassen lassen und sich dort aufgepäppelt, um dann zu seiner Familie in die SBZ (Sowjetisch besetzte Zone) zu fahren. Das fiel ihm bestimmt sehr schwer, ahnte er doch, was ihn erwartete. Aber zunächst sah er keinen Weg, seine Familie in den Westen zu holen. Für meinen jüngeren Bruder und mich war unser Vater ein fremder Mann und mein Bruder fragte meine Mutter, 'wann geht der fremde Mann denn wieder?' Auch wir waren unserem Vater fremd und er erlebte dasselbe Schicksal wie so viele Kriegsheimkehrer: Wie sollten sie ihren Platz in ihrer Familie wieder finden und einnehmen? Die Kinder waren ihnen fremd, die ältesten Söhne hatten oft den Platz des abwesenden Vaters eingenommen und akzeptierten dessen Autorität nicht mehr und auch die Frauen waren selbstständiger geworden und gingen nicht in ihre alte Rolle zurück. Wir haben nie mehr eine enge Beziehung zu unserem Vater aufbauen können und wohl auch deswegen freute er sich so sehr über die Geburt meiner kleinen Schwester 1953, sah er doch da eine neue Chance. Für unsere Mutter war es mit fast 44 Jahren kein Glücksfall und ich machte mir mit meinen 13 Jahren Gedanken, wo wir wohl einen Kinderwagen herbekämen?

Die Familie zog dann berufsbedingt 1948 in einen Nachbarort. Am siebenten Oktober 1949 wurde die Deutsche Demokratische Republik (DDR) gegründet. Mein Vater trug sich wohl schon länger mit dem Gedanken zu fliehen und im Oktober 1950 war es so weit. Meine ältere Schwester wurde vorübergehend zu Verwandten nach Sachsen geschickt, von wo sie dann später nach Berlin reiste. Wir fuhren mit dem Nötigsten nach Ost-Berlin und von dort mit der S-Bahn nach West-Berlin, wo wir alle bei einer bekannten Familie in Zehlendorf unterkamen. Das war für meine Mutter sehr, sehr schwer, hatte sie doch allen Besitz zurücklassen müssen und vor allem bedauerte sie auch die viele Arbeit, die sie mit dem Einwecken von 400 Gläsern Obst gehabt hatte. Die blieben nun auch in dem Haus zurück.

149

Einzelne Sachen wie Betten und Kleidung und die Nähmaschine kamen über Bekannte nach Kleinmachnow bei Berlin, wo wir sie nach und nach holen konnten. Wir wurden als politische Flüchtlinge anerkannt. Auch bekamen wir bald eine kleine Dachwohnung, wo wir mit sieben Personen und einem Untermieter, genannt Kostgänger (also mit voller Versorgung), wohnten, bis dann 1953 meine jüngste Schwester geboren wurde und für den Untermieter kein Platz mehr war.

Mein Vater konnte beruflich nicht mehr richtig Fuss fassen und erkrankte 1954/55 schwer an Krebs. Er starb im März 1956 im Alter von 53 Jahren. Nun war unsere Mutter wieder allein mit vier Kindern, denn mein ältester Bruder war inzwischen nach Canada ausgewandert und meine älteste Schwester in der Ausbildung zur Rot-Kreuz-Krankenschwester in Seesen im Harz. So blieben meine zwei Brüder, meine kleine Schwester und ich mit meiner Mutter zurück und wir konnten nun auch endlich in eine Sozial-Mietwohnung ziehen, eine „eigene" Wohnung, ohne fremde Menschen, wenn auch weiter sehr klein und beengt. Meine Mutter wurde 91 Jahre alt und hat ihr schweres Leben ohne Klagen und in grosser Bescheidenheit gemeistert. In ihrer Gelassenheit und ihrem stillen Mut war sie uns allen ein Vorbild. Sie starb im Jahre 2000.

Welche Gefühle verbinde ich mit der Kindheit im Krieg, der Nachkriegszeit, dem Hunger, der Flucht und den schwierigen Anfangsjahren in Berlin, das ja auch lange ein Trümmerfeld war? Wahrscheinlich habe ich, wie viele andere, vieles verdrängt. Natürlich war es auch eine schöne Kindheit, in einer kleinen Stadt, einem schönen Garten, in der Geborgenheit der Familie, auch wenn der Vater die ersten sieben Jahre fehlte, und mit den Geschwistern. Wohl auch daher habe ich eine besonders enge Bindung zu meiner Mutter gehabt. Aber da war auch viel Angst -

auch wenn der Krieg erst fern schien - um den abwesenden Vater, die Angst der Erwachsenen, die sie vor den Kindern zu verbergen versuchten und die sich wohl schon während meiner Geburt auf mich übertragen hat. Heute weiss man, wie schnell das geht, und auch die irrige Idee, dass Kinder ja noch nicht viel mitbekommen, hat sich als Trost aufgelöst. Wir redeten nicht darüber, über die Angst, mit den Eltern schon gar nicht und mit den Geschwistern auch nicht. Meine Brüder kannten keine Angst: 'Das war eben so.'

Erst jetzt denke ich anders darüber nach. Auch mein Mann, der 1938 in Ostpreussen geboren wurde und mit Mutter und Schwester im Januar/Februar 1945 über das zugefrorene Haff zu Verwandten nach Berlin fliehen konnte, 'erinnert' sich nicht. Die Familie redete auch nicht. Als sein Vater, der an der Ostfront und dann in russischer Gefangenschaft gewesen war, wiederkam, war auch er ein fremder Mann, und da sich die Eltern dann scheiden liessen, hatte er auch wenig Gelegenheit, seinen Vater überhaupt kennen zu lernen geschweige denn zu befragen.

Eine meiner Schwägerinnen wurde 1936 als drittes von fünf Kindern in Pommern geboren. Der Vater fiel im Krieg, der Grossvater, die Mutter und die fünf Kinder flüchteten kurz vor Kriegsende aus Pommern zu Verwandten nach Berlin. Die Mutter starb auf der Flucht, der kleine Bruder als Baby ein halbes Jahr später. Eine Grosstante zog die vier Kinder auf. Auch hier wurde nicht gesprochen.

Und wenn wir gefragt hätten? Hätten wir eine Antwort bekommen? Und hätten wir sie hören wollen? Heute weiss man, dass das miteinander Sprechen sehr wichtig ist, tragen sich doch die Kriegstraumata der Kriegskinder-Generation in die nächsten Generationen stumm weiter. Aber unsere Eltern und auch wir wussten es nicht anders. Es ging ums Überleben, um den Wicderaufbau und das Vergessen - auch der Tragweite der Schuld und Scham, wenn auch nicht einzelner, so doch des ganzen Volkes. Also ist es gut, dass wir jetzt anfangen zu sprechen.

Erikas Erinnerungen

Noch war 'Frieden' - aber es zündelte schon an vielen Ecken, als ich im Februar 1939 in Berlin-Steglitz (siehe Karte 6 für die wichtigsten im Text erwähnten Orte) geboren wurde. Am ersten September 1939 brach der Krieg aus, und noch im gleichen Monat wurde ich mit Kinderlähmung in die Charité eingeliefert - ein Schock für meine Eltern. Viele der jungen Ärzte hatten bereits ihre Einberufung an die Front erhalten, und es herrschte ein ziemliches Chaos - nach Aussage meiner Eltern.

Die ersten Kriegsjahre verbrachten wir in Berlin - somit auch die ersten Fliegerangriffe auf die Stadt. Bei Alarm - meistens nachts - musste alles sehr schnell gehen: ich wurde aus dem Bett geholt, bekam mein 'Überlebensköfferchen' in die Hand und ab ging es in den Luftschutzkeller im Haus, wo sich dann alle Bewohner versammelten. Dieser Keller in dem alten Berliner Haus war so verwinkelt - daran kann ich mich gut erinnern - dass mancher Zweifel aufkam, ob man uns denn im Falle eines Bombentreffers auf das Haus auch finden würde.

Ende 1942 wurden wir evakuiert - es ging nach Cottbus zu den Grosseltern väterlicherseits. Da meine Grossmutter mütterlicherseits bei uns lebte, standen nun drei Personen in der Wohnung, die untergebracht werden sollten. Mein Vater arbeitete in der Generaldirektion der damaligen Deutschen Reichsbahn in Berlin-Mitte. Er war 'uk' (unabkömmlich) gestellt und musste deshalb nicht in den Krieg sondern in Berlin die Stellung halten. Anfang 1945 wurde er doch noch zum 'Volkssturm' eingezogen. Diese 'Heimatfront' bestand hauptsächlich aus alten Männern.

In der Wohnung in Cottbus war eine drangvolle Enge, und es gab Schwierigkeiten im täglichen Zusammenleben. Meine Mutter war schwanger, und im April 1943 kam meine Schwester unter schwierigsten Bedingungen zur Welt. Nach einem schweren Luftangriff auf Cottbus zogen wir weiter nach Calbe an der Saale in das Haus des Bruders meines Vaters. Der Bruder war an der Front, und die gesamte Familie (Omas, Opas etc.,) versammelte sich nun dort. Wir, d.h. Mutter, Grossmutter und zwei Kinder, wurden in einem Lagerraum des ehemaligen Lebensmittelladens des Onkels einquartiert - zwischen Gurken- und Heringsfässern - natürlich war der Raum nicht heizbar und entsprechend kalt. Wir waren nicht gerade erwünscht - die Gründe dafür habe ich erst sehr viel später erfahren. Ich kann mich an viele Einzelheiten der Zurückweisung erinnern.

Wir lebten dort unter sehr schlechten Umständen bis zum Kriegsende. Erst kamen die Amerikaner, dann die Russen. Die errichteten Strassensperren wurden kurzerhand von den Panzern überrollt - für uns Kinder ein grosses Ereignis. Es herrschte strenge Ausgangssperre. Hielt sich jemand nicht daran, wurde er von den Russen mitgenommen und festgesetzt. Manch einer verschwand auch auf Nimmerwiedersehen.

Nach der Kapitulation am 8. Mai 1945 wurden alle Flüchtlinge angewiesen, binnen fünf Tagen an ihren ursprünglichen Wohnort zurückzukehren - egal, ob sie dort noch eine Wohnmöglichkeit hatten oder nicht. Mein Vater kam aus Berlin, um uns abzuholen. Unter abenteuerlichen Umständen erreichten wir unsere Wohnung in Berlin-Steglitz. Das Haus stand noch und unsere Wohnung war trotz Bombenschäden einigermassen bewohnbar, und wir richteten uns so gut es ging ein. Es gab nichts, weder zu Essen noch zu heizen. Der Schwarzmarkt blühte - wer noch etwas besass, ging dorthin, um es gegen Essen einzutauschen. Mutter und Grossmutter fuhren auf Hamstertour in total überfüllten Zügen in die Umgebung Berlins. Das taten natürlich noch viele tausend Berliner, und bald gab es nichts mehr zu hamstern.

Meine Eltern besassen ein Grundstück in Blankenfelde, südlich von Berlin. Sobald die S-Bahnen wieder fuhren, konnte meine Grossmutter dort den Garten bestellen, und die Versorgungslage entspannte sich etwas. Auf dem Balkon in Steglitz wuchsen inzwischen Tomaten. Karnickel gab es später auch - Grossmutter organisierte sie irgendwoher. Das Leben bestand hauptsächlich aus 'organisieren'.

Die Trümmer der zerstörten Häuser gehörten zum Alltag, ebenso die Gräber der eilig bestatteten Menschen in den Vorgärten, die kleinen Holzkreuze mit Stahlhelm, wenn dort ein Soldat bei den letzten Kämpfen um Berlin gefallen war - für mich eine schreckliche Erinnerung.

Im Herbst wurde ich eingeschult - mit zwei-wöchiger Verspätung - weil keiner in dem herrschenden Durcheinander mitbekommen hatte, dass die Schule begonnen hatte. Zu gleicher Zeit wurde die Behandlung meines halbgelähmten Poliobeins im Oskar-Helene-Heim wieder aufgenommen.

Trotz strengen Verbotes spielten wir Kinder gar zu gern in den umliegenden Ruinen, besonders in den halbzerbombten Villen in Berlin-Dahlem. Bis auf eine heftige Verletzung an meiner rechten Hand ging aber alles gut.

Mein Vater konnte 1945 weiter in seiner alten Dienststelle bleiben. Er hatte es geschafft, trotz Beamtenstatus nicht in die NSDAP einzutreten. So hatten wir unseren Vater und Ernährer, und waren dafür sehr dankbar. Steglitz wurde in der Vier-

155

Sektorenstadt Berlin amerikanischer Sektor. Da Vater in Ostberlin arbeitete, gab es nur Ostgeld. Nur einen winzigen Teil durfte er 1:1 in Westgeld umtauschen. So fuhr ich jeden zweiten Tag mit der S-Bahn zur Friedrichstrasse, um Brot und anderes für Ostgeld einzukaufen. Oft gab es aber nichts und ich musste ohne etwas eingekauft zu haben wieder heimfahren.

Der Hunger hinterliess seine Spuren: Mutter bekam eine offene Tbc und war viele Monate sehr krank. Ich wurde jeden zweiten Tag mit einem von Oma gekochten warmen Essen ins Krankenhaus am Heidelberger Platz geschickt. Da ich aber nicht zu meiner Mutter durfte, musste ich den Topf mit Inhalt an der Pforte abgeben. Wir hofften sehr, dass sie das Essen auch bekam. Wir nahmen noch ein junges Mädchen aus Schlesien auf, das Eltern und Heimat verloren hatte.

Dann kam der nächste Schlag: die Sowjets machten die Grenzen dicht, d.h. Westberlin war von der Versorgung abgeschnitten (die Berliner Blockade). Die Alliierten richteten die Luftbrücke ein: alle zwei Minuten kamen die ‚Rosinenbomber‘, Amerikaner und Briten flogen nach Tempelhof, später flogen auch die Franzosen nach Gatow und Tegel. Die zweieinhalb Millionen Westberliner wurden komplett mit Lebensmitteln – alles in Dosen – versorgt. Sogar Kohle wurde eingeflogen, um notdürftig die Kraftwerke in Westberlin am Laufen zu halten. Trotzdem gab es immer wieder Stromsperren, zu allen möglichen und unmöglichen Zeiten. Die russische Absperrung dauerte genau vom 24.6.1948 bis 12.5.1949, also fast ein ganzes Jahr. Meine kleine Schwester erkrankte ebenfalls an Tbc und wurde mit einem Kohleflugzeug nach Stuttgart zum Onkel ausgeflogen. Dort blieb sie ein ganzes Jahr. Mutter im Krankenhaus und die Schwester fort, das war für mich eine schlimme Zeit. Dann kam eines Tages Vater nicht vom Dienst in Ostberlin zurück. Keiner wusste, was passiert war. Nach drei Tagen voller Ungewissheit kam er wieder: die Russen hatten das gesamte Dezernat nach Karlshorst, einem östlichen Stadtteil von Berlin, ins russische Hauptquartier gebracht. Warum, wusste niemand.

Nach dem Ende der Luftbrücke konnten wir wieder in unseren Garten, und das Leben begann sich zu normalisieren. Vater züchtete Bienen und es gab sogar Honig!

Etwa um diese Zeit, ich war inzwischen Oberschülerin, machten wir einen Schulausflug zum Funkturm. Ich bekam das Fahrgeld für die U-Bahn abgezählt von zuhause mit. Da ich aber unbedingt auf den Funkturm wollte, nahm ich das Geld für die Rückfahrt und fuhr hinauf. Die Fahrt nach Hause machte ich sehr bequem in einem Jeep der französischen Streitkräfte, den ich einfach anhielt. Ein bisschen Französisch konnte ich schon, und die netten Soldaten brachten mich nach Steglitz - bis vor die Haustür. Oben auf dem Balkon stand bereits meine Mutter: sie sah ihre Tochter aus dem Militärauto aussteigen und ich ahnte, was jetzt folgen würde: eine Riesenabreibung - das hat gesessen! Seitdem bin ich nie wieder per Anhalter gefahren.

Im Mai 1952 war mit dem Garten endgültig Schluss: da er in der sogenannten 'Zone' lag, zwei km hinter Lichtenrade, der Sektorengrenze, durften Westberliner nicht mehr dorthin. (Erst im März 1990 - nach der 'Wende' - sah ich unseren Garten wieder.)

Die Situation Ost-West spitzte sich weiter zu - die Familie wurde unter Druck gesetzt, nach Ostberlin umzusiedeln. Eines Tages fand mein Vater seinen Schreibtisch durchwühlt vor und beschloss, nicht mehr in seine Dienststelle zurückzukehren: es war ihm zu gefährlich geworden. Nach einer kurzen Zeit der Arbeitslosigkeit bekam er im Bundesbahnzentralamt in Minden in Westfalen wieder eine Anstellung. Im Sommer 1953 verliessen wir Berlin und unsere schöne Wohnung und zogen nach Minden um. Ich musste meine geliebte Schule verlassen und auch alle Freundinnen – mit 14 Jahren war das schwer. Meine Schwester und ich wurden in den Zug gesetzt nach Helmstedt, dort wurden wir vom Vater erwartet. Die Fahrt von Berlin nach Helmstedt dauerte neun Stunden durch die 'Zone', oft unterbrochen von Kontrollen durch die Volkspolizei der DDR. Meine Mutter war mit dem Umzugswagen unterwegs - es wurde alles genau kontrolliert - bis auf den letzten Löffel.

An die Mindener Zeit habe ich keine guten Erinnerungen, besonders schlimm war die neue Schule. Als sogenanntes 'Flüchtlingskind' wurde man gemobbt, wie man heute sagen würde. Das Motto war: geht doch wieder dahin, wo ihr hergekommen seid. Unser Geschichtsunterricht endete mit dem Jahr 1918! Selbst die 'goldenen 20er Jahre' der Weimarer Republik kamen nicht vor, geschweige denn das '1000-jährige Reich'. Nach der mittleren Reife habe ich diese Schule verlassen. Die Wartezeit, bis ich mit 17 Jahren im Lettehaus meine Ausbildung zur Technischen Assistentin beginnen konnte, füllte ich mit einem Jahr Höhere Handelsschule, um auch Steno- und Maschine-Schreiben zu lernen. Zum Sommersemester 1956 ging ich dann wieder nach Berlin. Ich wohnte in einem Zimmer zur Untermiete in unserem ehemaligen Haus in Steglitz.

Mein Vater hat die gesamten Kriegsjahre in Berlin verbracht und in seiner Dienststelle der damaligen Deutschen Reichsbahn gearbeitet und genau gewusst, was an der Front passierte. Er war, wohl im Gegensatz zu den meisten Vätern und zu meiner Mutter, immer bereit, mit mir über die Kriegs- und Nachkriegsjahre zu sprechen.

Helgas Erinnerungen

Am neunten März 1945 mussten wir unsere Heimat in Lauenburg in Pommern (siehe Karte 7 für die wichtigsten im Text erwähnten Orte) endgültig verlassen. Ein paar Wochen vorher standen wir schon einmal auf der Landstrasse und sollten von Soldaten nach Danzig gebracht werden, um mit der 'Gustloff' das Land zu verlassen. Als wir nach Stunden durchgefroren waren, ohne dass ein Militärauto kam, sind wir wieder nach Hause gegangen. Das war wohl unser Glück.

Dieses Mal wurden wir von einem Lazarettzug voller Verwundeter aufgenommen. Die Soldaten hatten nichts mehr zu essen, deshalb bat man meine Mutter und ihre Freundin, aus ihren Kellern Eingemachtes und Wein zu holen. Der Zug würde noch eine Weile am Bahnhof stehen. Meine Tante, eine Schwester meiner Mutter, blieb bei uns Kindern. Ich war damals neun Jahre alt, meine Schwestern zehn und sechs.

Nach einer Weile wurde der Zug auf den Güterbahnhof rangiert. Wir hatten Angst, dass unsere Mütter uns nicht finden würden, sind immer wieder aus dem Zug gestiegen und haben gerufen. Die Bahnhöfe waren wegen der Bombenangriffe ohne Beleuchtung.

Von Ferne hörten wir schon die russische Front anrollen, und der Himmel über Danzig war rot von den Bränden. Zwei Tage später waren die Russen in Lauenburg. Nach Stunden voller Angst trafen unsere Mütter mit dem Proviant für die Soldaten ein. Niemand hatte ihnen auf dem Bahnhof sagen können, wo unser Zug gelandet war.

Wir wurden erst einmal nach Danzig-Neufahrwasser in ein geräumiges Kinderheim gebracht. Ein Bombenangriff in der Nacht versetzte uns in Angst und Schrecken. Es pfiff und dröhnte, die Fensterscheiben zersprangen und wir Kinder krochen unter die Tische im Tagesraum. Es war einfach schrecklich. In Lauenburg hatten wir auch Angriffe im Luftschutzkeller erlebt, aber die Bomber flogen über unsere Stadt hinweg nach Danzig. Nach dem Angriff wurden wir morgens in die Schiffshallen in 'Gotenhafen' Gdingen gebracht. Dort lagen wir auf Stroh und warteten auf das Schiff.

Endlich war es soweit! Mit der 'Mars' sollten wir nach Dänemark, das von den Deutschen besetzt war. Minensuchboote mussten immer erst freie Fahrt geben, weil die Ostsee vermint war, und so dauerte die Fahrt ein paar Tage. Die Verpflegung wurde knapp. Schiffszwieback wurde verteilt, das sind dicke, runde Kekse. Wir freuten uns, aber meine Schwester Eva entdeckte, dass die Kekse voller Maden waren. Wir haben trotzdem versucht, darum herum zu beissen. Vor den Toiletten wurde es immer voller, von jeder Familie stand immer einer in der Schlange, damit es schneller ging, wenn einer Bauchweh bekam. Viele waren schon krank. Dass die 'Gustloff' untergegangen war, wussten wir, und die Angst, dass wir ertrinken könnten, war gross.

In Kopenhagen brachte man uns erst in Schulen unter, mehrere Familien in einem Klassenraum. Strohsäcke dienten zum Schlafen. Regelmässig fanden Entlausungen statt. An alles kann ich mich nicht mehr erinnern. Unsere Mütter und andere Frauen veranstalteten 'bunte Abende' mit Vorträgen, Liedern und Klavierspiel in der Aula. Ich erinnere mich sogar an einen Seiltänzer auf dem Schulhof.

An Ruhr erkrankten viele Kinder, die sanitären Einrichtungen waren katastrophal, und diese Darmerkrankung griff um sich. Ich erkrankte ebenfalls und war tagelang bewusstlos. Das Bild vergesse ich nie, wie eine Mutter ihr totes, zweijähriges Kind nicht hergeben wollte und schreiend durch die Flure lief, das Kind auf dem Arm.

Am achten Mai 1945, dem Tag der Kapitulation, hörten wir plötzlich Schüsse auf dem Schulhof. Dänische Nazis schossen auf dänische Freiheitskämpfer, ein Mann wurde dabei getötet. Wir durften nicht an die Fenster und mussten in den Schulräumen bleiben, bis alles vorbei war.

Wir glaubten, nun bald in unsere Heimat zurückzukehren, aber Deutschland war zerstört. Es gab keinen Wohnraum und nicht genug Lebensmittel, um uns aufzunehmen. Dänemark hat die deutschen Flüchtlinge, etwa 250 000 sollen es gewesen sein, von 1945 – 1949 ernährt.

In Kopenhagen konnten wir nicht länger in den Schulen bleiben. Die deutschen Soldaten waren aus dem besetzten Land abgezogen und die Barackenlager wurden nun mit Flüchtlingen belegt. Wir aus Kopenhagen wurden per Schiff nach Jütland gebracht. Aalberg war ein ehemaliges Flughafengelände. Die Baracken, in denen wir unterkamen, waren völlig verwanzt. Ab und zu wurden sie mit Chemie ausgespritzt, dann mussten wir die zweistöckigen Betten nach draussen schaffen. Zum Zudecken bekamen wir Decken aus braunem Krepppapier mit Zellstoff gefüllt, so eine Art Steppdecke. Nachts hörten wir, wenn die Wanzen sich auf die Papierdecken fallen liessen und hatten schon Angst vor den Stichen. Es gab dann hässliche, juckende Beulen.

Das Lager war ziemlich gross. Wir hatten auch Schulunterricht, mehrere Jahrgänge zusammen. Der Weg zur Schule war oft eine Plage, denn dort gab es viele Sandstürme und im Winter Schneestürme. Den Unterricht hielt ein kleinwüchsiger Studienrat, bei dem wir viel lernten. Einige Männer, die kriegsuntauglich oder zu alt waren, befanden sich unter den Flüchtlingen.

In der Baracke waren drei bis vier Familien in einem Raum. Wir teilten unsere Bereiche mit Leinen auf, auf die wir graue Decken (aus Militärbestand) hängten. Geheizt haben wir im Winter mit Torf in einem Kanonenofen. Das Rohr führte durchs Fenster nach draussen. Der Torf wurde uns zugeteilt, und weil wir oft froren, haben unsere Mütter einmal Torf geklaut, das in einer Halle lagerte. Sie wurden natürlich geschnappt und mussten ein paar Stunden ins Lagergefängnis. Das war uns sehr peinlich.

Um unser Lager war Stacheldraht. In einem offenen Hochsitz wurden wir von Dänen bewacht. Zwei Bewacher waren immer sehr freundlich und brachten uns öfter Leckerei mit. Einer schenkte mir mal ein rotkariertes Taschentuch, weil meine Nase lief; das habe ich noch Jahrzehnte aufgehoben. Wir Kinder hatten ja kaum etwas Eigenes. Unser Spielzeug, unsere Puppen, alles mussten wir zu Hause lassen. Wir zogen mit Rucksäcken, die unsere Mutter aus Leinenhandtüchern genäht hatte, los, und da war nur das Nötigste drin.

In den zweieinhalb Jahren Flüchtlingslager wuchsen wir aus unseren Schuhen und Kleidern heraus. Alte Männer, die bei uns im Lager waren, schnitzten Holzpantinen für uns. Kleider wurden aus Bettbezügen (kariert, auch aus Militärbeständen) mit der Hand genäht. Einige Mädchen, darunter auch ich, haben mit einer einfachen Holzspindel Fäden aus Watte gesponnen. Aus dem Garn und den herausgezogenen Fäden von rot-braunen Sesselbezügen wurden Pullover gestrickt, und aus Verbandsmull, das wir in Streifen schnitten, Frotteepullover! Die waren natürlich steif wie ein Brett.

Die Frauen im Lager waren oft verzweifelt, weil sie nichts von ihren Angehörigen in Deutschland hörten und von den Männern, ob sie in Gefangenschaft waren, ob sie noch lebten. Manche erhielten Nachricht und waren glücklich, andere liessen sich wahrsagen, um ein bisschen Hoffnung zu haben.

Wer in Deutschland eine Wohnung nachweisen konnte, durfte Dänemark mit einem Transport verlassen. Kriegerwitwen und Kinder kamen nach Westdeutschland. Meine Mutter wusste nicht, dass mein Vater schon im April 1945 gefallen war. Sie wollte aber unbedingt zurück nach Deutschland, um etwas zu erfahren. Durch eine Freundin erhielt sie eine Zuzugsgenehmigung nach Sonneberg in Thüringen. Meine Tante, Vaters Schwester, traute sich nicht, meiner Mutter vom Tod meines Vaters zu berichten, aus Angst, sie könnte sich das Leben nehmen, wie es viele im Lager taten.

So kamen wir im August 1947 mit einem Transport nach Deutschland, erst mit einem Schiff, dann mit der Bahn. Die dänische Regierung hatte einen Waggon mit Getreide für Deutschland mitgegeben, der hinter der Lokomotive war, dahinter gleich unser Gepäck. In der Nähe von Stralsund war plötzlich Feuer. Die Wagen hinter der Lok brannten lichterloh! Wir rannten alle aus dem Zug. Nun besassen wir nur noch das, was wir auf dem Leib trugen. Der Brand soll durch Feuerfunken ausgelöst worden sein, man sprach auch von Sabotage.

In Eggesin, in Mecklenburg, wurden wir in Wochenendhäusern untergebracht. Wir mussten dort einige Zeit in Quarantäne bleiben. Dort befanden sich russische Besatzungssoldaten. Einige junge Mädchen hatten am Tag mit den Russen geflirtet. Nachts kamen die betrunkenen Soldaten, und weil sie nicht an die Mädchen herankamen, schlugen sie Türen und Fenster ein und schrien laut. Wir haben uns in den Räumen verbarrikadiert und wieder einmal vor Angst gezittert.

Unsere geretteten, aber angesengten Sachen aus dem Zug wurden auf einem grossen Platz ausgerufen. Die Eigentümer kamen nicht immer zu ihrem Besitz; manchmal meldeten mehrere Personen Anspruch darauf an. Es kam zu Streitereien und unschönen Szenen. Lange rochen unsere Kleider nach dem überstandenen Brand.

Nach der Quarantäne-Zeit kamen wir in die Orte, für die wir Zuzugsgenehmigungen hatten. Meine Mutter und wir drei Schwestern erhielten ein Zimmer bei einem Fleischer und Gastwirt in Sonneberg in Thüringen. In dem einen Zimmer haben wir gewohnt, geschlafen, gekocht und Schularbeiten gemacht.

Das Jahr 1947 war in der damaligen Ostzone ein Hungerjahr, vor allem für die Menschen, die keinen Garten hatten und nichts von ihrem Besitz eintauschen konnten. Meine Mutter bekam Arbeit in einer Bekleidungsfabrik. Eva und ich gingen nach der Schule zum 'Hamstern' aufs Land. Wir waren glücklich, wenn wir mit drei Kartoffeln und ein paar Scheiben Brot nach Hause kamen. Wir hatten immer Bauchweh und nachts träumten wir von riesigen Torten, die aber nach nichts schmeckten. Nach der Ernte sammelten wir Felder ab.

165

Meine jüngste Schwester Renate musste nach der Bahnfahrt von Dänemark mit einem Blinddarmdurchbruch ins Krankenhaus. Meine Mutter schob sie in einem Sportwagen (sie war acht Jahre alt) den langen Weg hin zum Krankenhaus. Einen Krankenwagen gab es nicht. Wenn wir sie besuchten, hatte sie immer ein Stück Brot mit Leberwurst, die sie nicht mochte, in ihrer Nachttischschublade. Darunter stand das Nachtgeschirr.

Durch das Rote Kreuz fanden wir nach und nach Verwandte und Freunde wieder, darunter auch ein älteres Ehepaar aus unserer Heimat, deren Sohn gefallen war. Da ich zu der Zeit mit 13 Jahren nur 24 kg wog, wurde ich von ihnen eingeladen, in den Schulferien zu kommen um mich zu erholen.

Ich wurde von 'Schleusern', die meine Mutter bezahlte, bei Nacht und Nebel über die damals noch 'grüne' Grenze nach Westdeutschland gebracht. Am Bahnhof in Neustadt wurde ich von der Bahnpolizei geschnappt, als ich meine nassen Socken mit trockenen wechselte. Da ich bitterlich weinte, hatten sie Mitleid mit mir und beförderten mich im 'Dienstwagen' nach Höxter an der Weser. Da sassen amerikanische Soldaten und assen fett gebackene Berliner Pfannkuchen und Erdnüsse. Ich habe wohl nur darauf gestarrt, denn als sie ausstiegen, warfen sie mir die Tüten mit den Resten auf den Schoss.

Da ich in den nächsten Tagen von der Ernährungsumstellung einen Wasserbauch bekam, ging die Tante (wie ich sie nannte) mit mir zum Arzt. Ich bekam dann erst mal Diät: Haferbrei, den ich heute noch gerne esse! Mir wurde angeboten, in Höxter bei dem Ehepaar zu bleiben und die Schulausbildung dort zu beenden.

Meine Mutter und meine Schwestern habe ich lange nicht sehen können, da die Grenzen immer dichter wurden und Sonneberg zum Sperrgebiet erklärt wurde. Wir waren glücklich, als die Reisemöglichkeiten gelockert wurden und dann, in 1989, noch die Mauer fiel. Die Jahre der Trennung waren für beide Seiten nicht einfach.

Henriettes Erinnerungen

Am 1.11.1937 wurde ich als zweites Kind meiner Eltern in Perleberg (siehe Karte 8 für die wichtigsten im Text erwähnten Orte) geboren. Mein Bruder war zwei Jahre älter. 1941 wurde dann noch eine Schwester geboren. Perleberg ist eine Kreisstadt im Nordwesten von Brandenburg und war seit Kaisers Zeiten Garnisonstadt. Wir wohnten in einem von den Grosseltern väterlicherseits geerbten Zweifamilienhaus. Es lag auf einem grossen Grundstück mit noch einem Mietshaus und Gewerberäumen meines Vaters, der wie sein Vater Malermeister war.

In den ersten Kriegsjahren musste das Gewerbe schon abgemeldet werden, die Gesellen wurden eingezogen und mein Vater als Soldat zur Flugwache in Perleberg einberufen. Nahe bei der Stadt lag auch ein Flugplatz, ehemals für Segelflieger errichtet. Irgendwann kam mein Vater nach Pinneberg bei Hamburg, wurde dort zum Funker ausgebildet und danach in Richtung Osten versetzt, aber nicht direkt an die Front. Er musste in der Etappe Zeichnungen über Luftbewegungen anfertigen.

In Perleberg selber fiel nur eine Bombe, wahrscheinlich aus Versehen, doch es gab zahlreiche Angriffe auf den Flughafen. Über unsere Köpfe hinweg flogen sehr viele Bombergeschwader immer in Richtung Berlin. So lebten wir in den letzten Kriegsjahren ständig mit Fliegeralarm. Oftmals mussten wir auch in der Schule in einen Schutzkeller oder gingen zu Hause mit allen Mietern vom Hinterhof in den Hauskeller. An der Kellertür stand in grosser Schrift: 'Als Schutzraum geeignet für 15 Personen' (wie beruhigend).

Nachts war es schrecklich, in den Keller zu müssen, mein Bruder weigerte sich oft.

Nahrungsmittel gab es wohl immer noch genug. Meine Grosseltern mütterlicherseits hatten unten im Haus einen Kleinstladen, abgetrennt vom Wohnzimmer. Mein Grossvater war Kriegsinvalide vom 1.Weltkrieg, und so verdiente man sich zur Rente noch etwas dazu. Sie verkauften Butter, Käse und Quark, natürlich gegen Lebensmittelmarken. Wenn der Molkereibesitzer vom Lande jeden Freitag Ware lieferte, bekamen wir Kinder von unserer Oma Quark, gerührt mit Marmelade oder Zucker. 'Quark macht stark, Quark alleene macht krumme Beene' sagte sie immer mit glücklichem Gesicht. Wir hatten auch einen Garten mit Obstbäumen und angebautem Gemüse, wie wertvoll in diesen schlechten Zeiten!

Zu einer Familie hinten im Mietshaus kamen so etwa 1942 noch eine Tochter aus Berlin mit drei Söhnen, alle so alt wie wir Kinder. Sie waren evakuiert worden. Zu den Grosseltern im Vorderhaus zog meine Tante aus Berlin-Lankwitz mit ihrer zweijährigen Tochter, auch sie flohen vor den Bombenangriffen. Nun spielten viele Kinder auf unserem Grundstück, gut behütet von den Müttern. Ihre Ängste und Sorgen spürten wir Kinder nicht. Die Väter waren alle im Krieg!

Mit dem beginnenden Winter 1944/45 erreichten Perleberg die Trecks mit Flüchtlingen aus Ostpreussen. Sie zogen mit ihren bis hoch oben vollbepackten Pferdewagen ununterbrochen durch unsere Strasse, immer zur Elbbrücke bei Wittenberge, schon damals Richtung Westen! Manche machten auch Rast bei uns und unsere Mütter halfen, wo sie nur konnten. Mich haben die Trecks stark beeindruckt, Teppiche konnte man als Dach nutzen. Weiter waren sehr, sehr viele Decken enorm wichtig bei einer

Flucht. Noch heute schätze ich Wolldecken für alle Unternehmungen ausser Haus!

Nun bekamen wir den Krieg zu spüren. In der Nachbarschaft wurde das Haus einer Evangelischen Gemeinschaft zum Lazarett umfunktioniert. Wir Kinder, neugierig und ohne Berührungsängste, sahen ängstlich und voller Mitleid, wie die Verletzten in den grossen Saal transportiert wurden. Es waren wohl eher Leichtverletzte, und sie waren nur kurzzeitig dort stationiert, aber ihr Anblick erschütterte uns sehr.

Ab März-April 1945 wurde der Unterricht in den Schulen schwieriger, man brauchte die Räume für neue Flüchtlinge. Es gab auch immer öfter Fliegeralarm. In den Strassen wurden Panzersperren gebaut und uns Angst gemacht, dass die Panzer Frauen und Kinder einfach überrollen würden!

Für meine Mutter begann eine sehr harte Zeit. Sie war noch einmal schwanger geworden und der Geburtstermin lag bei Mitte April! Mein Vater wurde Anfang April von seinem Vorgesetzten aus Löbau in der Lausitz nach Hause geschickt, um einen Farbkompressor aus seiner Werkstatt zu holen, zum Tarnen von Militärfahrzeugen. Das noch im April 1945!

Wir sind heute überzeugt, dass es eine menschliche Geste von seinem Chef war, der annahm, dass Vater die Gelegenheit wohl nützen würde, um zu Hause bei seiner hochschwangeren Frau zu bleiben. Doch er fuhr pflichtbewusst und treu mit dem Gerät nach Löbau zurück. Ein Wagen hatte ihn an der Strasse abgeholt. Was für ein schwerer Abschied für meine Mutter, ich kann mich an diesen Tag noch genau erinnern.

Wir Kinder merkten nun doch, dass es ernst wurde, alle Erwachsenen waren hochgradig nervös, es gab die Gerüchte von der Wunderwaffe, aber meine Tante aus Berlin blieb da sehr realistisch und nahm uns den Glauben daran.

In der Nacht vom 14. zum 15. April, als Potsdam zum Schluss noch flächendeckend bombardiert wurde, setzten bei meiner Mutter die Wehen ein. Wir anderen sassen alle im Luftschutzkeller und die Bomber flogen in grossen Verbänden über uns in Richtung Potsdam.

Meine arme Mutter lag im obersten Stockwerk im Schlafzimmer, aber ihre beiden Schwestern standen ihr bei. Die jüngste Schwester holte dann das kleine Mädchen auf die Welt. Später kam noch eine Hebamme dazu, und am Morgen durften wir dann unsere kleine Schwester bewundern. Es war alles gut gegangen, meine Mutter konnte zum Glück auch stillen und das Kind kam durch.

Die Angst aber wurde täglich grösser, irgendwie bereiteten wir uns darauf vor, auch noch fliehen zu müssen. In unsere Schulmappen kamen Windeln und Babywäsche, die Puppen mussten wieder raus. Zur Flucht kam es aber zum Glück nicht.

Am zweiten Mai 1945 marschierte der Russe dann in Perleberg ein. Die Stadt wurde kampflos übergeben. Aus dem Rathaus soll eine weisse Fahne gehangen haben. Wir sassen alle ängstlich im Keller und harrten der Dinge. Mein Grossvater war der einzige Mann, er musste noch einen Hitlerjungen durch Backpfeifen zurückholen, der uns auf der Strasse verteidigen wollte!! So sassen wir 10 Frauen und 14 Kinder und warteten ab. Voller Todesangst blickten wir auf die Kellertreppe, als ein grimmiger Mongole mit vorgehaltener Kalaschnikow die Treppe herunterkam und „URI URI" rief. Am ganzen Leib zitternd reichten ihm alle Frauen ihre Uhren und Schmuckstücke. Dabei beliess er es.

Abends gingen wir dann hoch in unsere Wohnung, blieben zusammen und bildeten eine Schutz- und Trutzgemeinschaft. Die Kinder wurden platt auf dem Fussboden zum Schlafen gelegt, darüber im Dachgeschoss hielten sich alle Frauen auf. Mein Grossvater war der Hüter der Kinder. Das war sehr geschickt, denn nachts kamen wieder Russen ins Haus. Als sie in den Wohnstuben die vielen Kinder und den Grossvater sahen, riefen sie: 'oh, so viele Kinder!' und verschwanden wieder. Die Frauen oben waren gerettet und wir auch. Am Vormittag darauf zerriss eine der Frauen ein Laken in Streifen, die wir um den Arm gebunden bekamen. Das sollte heissen: Wir haben uns ergeben! In den nächsten Tagen marschierten ununterbrochen Russen in die Stadt, abends durchsuchten sie dann Keller und leere Wohnungen nach Beutegut. Aus unserem Keller verschwanden neben Kleidung und Fotoapparaten auch etliche Gläser eingeweckter, tiefrot leuchtender Erdbeeren, zur Schadenfreude meiner Mutter. Sie hatte beim Einwecken zu viel rote Farbe benutzt und die Erdbeeren waren alle bitter!

Wir Kinder haben weitere Brutalitäten nicht mitbekommen, in der Innenstadt von Perleberg gab es aber schreckliche Szenen und manche Familien nahmen sich das Leben. In den folgenden Tagen durften sich dann einige Frauen in der Nähe der Kasernen nach Brot anstellen. Diese Aktion muss sehr bald angelaufen sein. Im Keller hatten wir von dem Warenlager des Ladens noch eine halbe Tonne Butter, ich weiss aber nicht, wie gross die Tonne überhaupt war. Jedenfalls rettete sie uns alle vor der ersten grossen Not. Eine Förstersfrau kochte Suppe aus Sauerampfer oder Brennnesseln. Alle Frauen waren äusserst erfinderisch beim Zubereiten der Mahlzeiten.

Schon im Mitte Mai 1945 kam unser Vater in Begleitung eines Polen nach Hause. Beide waren total zerlumpt, ausgehungert aber ansonsten körperlich unversehrt. Mein Vater hatte sich diesem Polen angeschlossen. Zu Fuss oder als Anhalter hatten sie die Strecke von Löbau in der Lausitz bis Perleberg zurückgelegt. Mein Vater stellte sich taubstumm und der Pole konnte russisch sprechen. Sie müssen einen Schutzengel gehabt haben! Die beiden Männer assen zum allergrössten Erstaunen von uns Kindern einen ganzen Eimer mit gekochten Kartoffeln leer. Wer weiss, was geschehen wäre, wenn sich mein Vater im April als Deserteur versteckt hätte!

Die anderen Frauen waren inzwischen auch in ihre Wohnungen zurückgekehrt. Jetzt hatten wir vier Kinder wieder einen Vater, der uns und unsere Mutter nun beschützte. Man holte ihn von der Sowjetischen Kommandantur in Perleberg zu Malerarbeiten, er galt als Spezialist für Autolackiererei. Der Kommandant hatte betrunken sein schönes Auto beschädigt, das mein Vater wieder fachgerecht ausbesserte. Danach folgten viele Aufträge. Als Lohn erhielt er Naturalien wie Mehl, sehr süsse Fondantbonbons und einmal sogar eine Ziege. Eines Nachts kam er mit einer Kuh am Strick nach Hause! Wir hätten auch einen Wiesenweg zum Grasen gehabt, aber sie musste zum Schlachthof, da sie Maul- und Klauenseuche hatte. Unser Traum von frischer Milch war damit geplatzt.

Um vor umher strolchenden Russen geschützt zu sein, gab der Kommandant meinem Vater ein Schreiben, mit Unterschrift und Stempel, dass in unserem Haus Typhus herrsche. Es kam unter Glas an die Tür, und kein Russe betrat mehr unser Haus. Vor dieser Krankheit hatten sie allergrösste Angst.

Im Sommer 1945 war es meine Aufgabe, jeden Abend zwei km zu Fuss mit einer Milchkanne in der Hand ins nächste Dorf zu wandern und um Milch für meine kleinste Schwester zu betteln. Mit mir pilgerten aber sehr viele Kinder und Erwachsene. Nicht immer waren wir erfolgreich. Im Sommer ernteten wir dann Äpfel, Birnen und Pflaumen aus dem Garten. Einen Teil nutzte man zum Tauschen. Ein Glück, dass die Grosseltern nach dem ersten Weltkrieg sehr viele Bäume angepflanzt hatten. So lernten wir Kinder sehr bald, wie man sich in der Not helfen muss!

Eines Tages brachte uns jemand einen Karton voller Mundharmonikas, höchstwahrscheinlich aus Plünderung. Vierzehn Kinder erhielten jeweils zwei bis drei Stück. Alle zusammen machten damit auf dem Hof natürlich Musik! Einer immer lauter als der andere! Unsere Mütter mussten starke Nerven haben!

Ab September begann wieder die Schule. Die Klassenstärke war riesig, 50-60 Schüler, es gab nur noch wenige Lehrer, einige mussten auch erst entnazifiziert werden. Der kalte Winter 1945/46 ist mir so in Erinnerung, dass wir tagsüber alle in einem Zimmer zusammen wohnten. Ein irgendwo erstandener kleiner eiserner Ofen war unser wichtigstes Gut. Das Haus hatte eigentlich eine Zentralheizung, doch die war stillgelegt. Schularbeiten wurden oft bei Stromsperre mit Kerzenlicht gemacht. Abends ging es dann in die eiskalten und klammen Federbetten.

Wir gehörten jetzt zur Sowjetischen Besatzungszone. In unserer Stadt verschwanden nach Kriegsende noch viele Personen, manche auf Nimmerwiedersehen, was nie aufgeklärt wurde. Es gab Denunziationen und viel Misstrauen gegenüber der Bevölkerung. Es herrschte wieder Angst. Dennoch machten sich die Davongekommenen an einen Wiederaufbau, wenn auch unter grössten Schwierigkeiten. Mein Vater eröffnete bald wieder seinen Betrieb, die meisten Gesellen kamen zu ihm zurück. Der von uns Kindern sehr geliebte Lehrling Fritz war mit dabei. Er blieb meinem Vater über das 50. Geschäftsjubiläum hinaus treu und lebt noch heute.

Die vier Schwiegersöhne meines Grossvaters waren im Krieg an verschiedenen Fronten. Sie sind alle aus Gefangenschaft in England und Amerika wieder nach Hause gekommen. Dieses Glück hat die Familien zusammengeschmiedet, sie haben sich später immer wieder besucht. Auch bei uns Cousinen gab es eine tiefe Verbundenheit durch das gemeinsam in Perleberg durchgestandene Kriegsende. Diese Verbundenheit hält bis heute an.

Im Schulunterricht in der DDR erfuhren wir sehr viel über die Nazizeit und ihre Gräueltaten. Der Widerstand der Arbeiterklasse, besonders der Kommunisten, wurde ausführlich in Wort und Bild, auch in Filmen, geschildert. Das führte zu Diskussionen mit unseren Eltern, die oft das bezweifelten, was wir berichteten. Die Väter schwiegen über ihre Kriegserlebnisse an der Front. Dass es auch noch einen bürgerlichen Widerstand gab, erfuhren wir erst viel später.

Gegen die anhaltende Mangelwirtschaft in der DDR setzten alle wieder ihre Erfahrungen aus den Nachkriegsjahren ein. Bis zum Schluss in 1989 gab es hier eine Tauschgesellschaft.

Nur ein grosser Wunsch war immer präsent: 'Nie wieder Krieg!'

Ingrids Erinnerungen

Geboren wurde ich 1937 in Leipzig (siehe Karte 9 für die wichtigsten im Text erwähnten Orte), dort wohnten wir in einem Eckhaus am Rosental mit riesigem Erker. In diesem Erkerzimmer wurden meine Schwester Christel und ich getauft. Als ich vier Jahre alt war bekam ich von meiner Mutter die erste Ohrfeige, die mir heute noch lebhaft im Gedächtnis ist. Wir mussten beim Einkaufen durch das Judenviertel laufen, sie durften nicht auf den Fusssteig, gingen gebückt mit dem Judenstern am Mantel auf der Strasse. Im Kindergarten hatte ich gelernt, dass sie ganz böse Menschen sind. Ich streckte ihnen deshalb die Zunge raus und machte eine lange Nase. Sofort bekam ich eine gewischt. Meine Mutter erklärte mir, dass das ganz liebe Leute sind, die aber verfolgt werden und dass man sich niemals Erwachsenen gegenüber so verhalten darf.

Wegen des Krieges zogen wir zu den Grosseltern ungefähr 40 km von Leipzig entfernt in die Kleinstadt Naunhof in eine grosse Wohnung. Unser Garten grenzte fast an den von Grossvater, wo wir Kinder ständig spielten. Da wir alle keine Uhr hatten, um zu den Mahlzeiten pünktlich zu sein, läutete Hedwig mit einer grossen Kuhglocke. Alle Kinder der Nachbarschaft mussten dann auch nach Hause. Wir nahmen alle Mahlzeiten mit der ganzen Familie ein. Die Erwachsenen waren sehr streng mit uns: wir mussten hinter den Stühlen stehen und warten bis die Grosseltern und Eltern sassen, danach kamen wir zum Sitzen. Wenn die Erwachsenen redeten, mussten wir Kinder schweigen.

Am 30. Mai 1941 wurde meine Schwester Andrea geboren. Unsere liebe Elly versorgte sie. Meine grosse Liebe galt unserm Airedaleterrier Falk, der mich schon immer bewacht hatte, als ich noch im Kinderwagen im Garten stand. Der Krieg wurde immer schlimmer und ich fürchtete mich vor den brennenden Häusern. Da meine Grossmutter und ihre Schwester völlig ausgebombt wurden und nichts retten konnten, fanden sie bei uns in Naunhof eine Bleibe.

Wir hatten einen grossen Sandkasten in dem wir spielten. Neben uns weideten drei Gänse. Plötzlich sah ich, wie sie alle gleichzeitig ihren Kopf nach dem Himmel verdrehten. Ich sagte es gleich meiner Mutter und wir entdeckten eine Blindgängerbombe am Fallschirm, die gerade auf den Bahndamm fiel. Sofort benachrichtigten wir die Polizei, die den Zug stoppte und die Bombe entschärfte. So haben die Gänse eine Katastrophe verhindert.

Ausser Gänsen hatten wir Hühner und Kaninchen, die wurden in einem Schuppen vor Dieben versteckt. Für mich war es schrecklich, wenn wieder eines geschlachtet werden musste, obwohl ich die warmen Kaninchenhandschuhe gern trug. Mein Grossvater war auch ein grosser Bienenzüchter. Wir hatten 12 Völker. Die Waben voller Honig stellten wir in die Handschleudermaschine und der Honig wurde gleich in Gläser gefüllt. Zum Schluss durften wir Nackedeie in die Schleuder klettern um die letzten Reste heraus zu lecken, ein Fest für die Kinder. Da wir dann überall klebten, wurden wir in die von der Sonne erwärmten Zinn-Regen-Wasserwannen gesteckt.

Mein Vater wurde in den Krieg als Marineartillerieoffizier eingezogen und diente in Cuxhaven. Der Krieg begann für uns mit Tieffliegerangriffen, manchmal mitten in der Nacht mussten wir in den Keller laufen. Am Tag drauf sammelten wir die leeren Patronenhülsen. Wegen der Granatsplitter baute Grossvater einen Erdbunker im Garten. Dort versteckte er später Juden, gab ihnen Geld, damit sie sich aus Deutschland retten konnten.

Damit wir etwas zu essen hatten, wurden nun statt Rasen Gemüsebeete angelegt. Wir Kinder lernten schon früh auf unseren eigenen Beeten den Anbau von Blumen und Gemüse. Da es keinen Dünger gab, hatten wir auf dem Rad immer eine Holzkiste und Schaufel, um Pferdeäpfel einzusammeln. Von den vielen Flüchtlingen, die 1944 kamen, nahmen wir Frau Wohlang mit ihrer Tochter Brigitte aus dem Sudetenland (deutsch-sprechende Teile der ehemaligen Tschechoslowakei) in unsere grosse Wohnung auf. Sie kochte von da an immer für uns und Brigitte, ein Jahr älter als ich, wurde unsere vierte Schwester.

Es gab langsam nichts mehr zu kaufen, die Lebensmittel wurden durch Lebensmittelmarken rationiert. Hin und wieder tauschten die Grosseltern Schmuck und Teppiche bei den Bauern für Milch, Mehl und Kartoffeln ein. Auch die Kohle-Briketts aus Steinkohle, später nur noch aus Braunkohle, wurden rationiert. Keine Zentralheizung konnte mehr betrieben werden. Es wurden Eisenöfen und ins Wohnzimmer ein kleiner Kachelofen gesetzt, die auch mit Holz geheizt werden konnten. Wir schleppten täglich Kohlen und sammelten im Wald ofenfertiges Holz. Mit einem Leiterwagen zogen wir los und tarnten oft die kleinen Stämme, denn nur eine bestimmte Dicke durfte gesammelt werden. Langsam wurde auch das rar, da jede Familie dieselbe Idee hatte.

Als Älteste fuhr ich sehr bald mit meiner Mutter zum Ährenlesen und später Kartoffelstoppeln. Ich hatte ein kleines Schürzchen mit einer grossen Tasche um, wo die Ähren hineinkamen. Es war mühsam, da die Bauern nicht mehr viel übrig liessen nach der Ernte. Das Korn wurde dann in einer Bodenkammer gelagert. Da wir Kinder immer Hunger hatten, entdeckten wir eines Tages den Schlüssel und assen das Korn roh. Mutter bemerkte es gleich und es gab Haue.

Zu Weihnachten bekamen wir Kinder jeder ein Pfund Brot, für uns das schönste Weihnachtsgeschenk. Täglich nach dem Frühstück bekamen wir jeder von den drei Grosseltern noch eine halbe Scheibe Brot, so wurde der Hunger etwas erträglicher. Bonbon oder Schokolade gab es nicht, auch keinen Zucker. Da es nichts zum Anziehen gab und wir immer grösser wurden, nähte uns Grossmutter aus der Kaiserfahne weiss rote Kleidchen. Das Schwarz wurde zu sehr kratzigen Turnhosen verwendet. So zerschnitt sie später auch die Hakenkreuzfahne, die wir alle hissen mussten an besonderen Tagen. Grossmutter war schon sehr fortschrittlich, sie hatte die erste elektrische Nähmaschine, bei unserer musste man noch mit den Füssen die Wippe treten.

Das schlimmste für uns Kinder war 1943 der Abschied von Elly, unserm Kindermädchen, wir konnten sie nicht mehr bezahlen. Falk, unser treuer Hund, wurde von den Gebirgsjägern als Lawinenhund ausgebildet. Er hat viele gerettet wurde uns später berichtet; ich habe tagelang geweint, wurde aber von meiner Grossmutter getröstet, dass er es viel besser hätte, denn wir hätten ihn nicht ernähren können.

Im Herbst 1943 begann der Ernst des Lebens: ich kam in die Schule. Stolz trug ich einen ledernen Schulranzen mit Schiefertafel, Griffel und Schwamm. In der Schule hatte ich nichts zu lachen, da ich immer die Grösste war.

Um für die Familie etwas zu verdienen, meldete ich mich gleich zum Kartoffeln lesen. Bei grosser Sommerhitze half ich auch noch beim Möhren verziehen auf dem Feld. Ausserdem mussten wir Schüler alle beim Kartoffelkäfer sammeln helfen. Im Winter hatten wir oft keine Schule, wegen Heizungs- und Strommangel. Grossmutter unterrichtete uns und die Nachbarskinder. Besonders gefiel mir Erdkunde, wenn sie uns von ihren Reisen erzählte oder den grossen Weltatlas aufschlug.

Als 1945 der Krieg endlich zu Ende war, steckte mein Vater in englischer Gefangenschaft. Nun kamen die Amerikaner. In grosser Eile wurden der Schmuck und die silbernen Bestecke unter dem Fahrradschuppen vergraben, denn wir hatten gehört, dass sie plünderten. Wir hatten grosse Angst, aber sie waren sehr nett. Da der Kommandant Liri sich das Haus der Grosseltern als seine Bleibe aussuchte, mussten wir ausziehen. Wir schliefen in einem anderen Haus alle in einem grossen Raum mit fremden Leuten zusammen, nur durch einen Paravent getrennt. Mutter konnte ein wenig Englisch und erreichte bei Liri, dass wir in unsere frühere Wohnung mit den Grosseltern und Oma zurück durften. Da die Amerikaner viel an Essen wegwarfen, holten wir uns Essbares vom Komposthaufen, denn wir durften auch nicht mehr aus dem Garten das Gemüse ernten. Vor unserem Küchenfenster bettelten wir Kinder manchmal und erhielten Schokolade.

Liri wollte uns dann mit Möbeln nach dem Westen oder in die USA mitnehmen, denn die Russen bekamen nun Sachsen. Wo sollte meine Mutter hin mit drei Kindern und mein Vater noch nicht frei? Die Frauen unseres Dorfes hatten alle Angst vor Vergewaltigungen von Russen. Liri bewirkte aber noch, dass in unserem Naunhof niemandem etwas geschah. Da die Amerikaner aus allen Häusern die Sachen über das ganze Dorf verteilt hatten, setzte eine wilde Jagd nach den eigenen Dingen ein. Auf den Marktplatz brachte jeder, was ihm nicht gehörte, und so bekamen wir den grössten Teil unserer Wäsche und Möbel zurück.

In der Schule bekamen wir nun Russisch-Unterricht. Wir hatten ganz junge, neue Lehrer. Es begann die Gründung der Jungen Pioniere. Kirchenbesuche wurden nicht gern gesehen. Statt Konfirmation wurde die Jugendweihe eingeführt. Wir drückten uns vor diesen kommunistischen Dingen.

1948 wurde Vater aus englischer Gefangenschaft entlassen. Er liess sich bei Freunden in Öderquart etwas aufpäppeln und zog dann nach Bielefeld, wo noch sehr viele Verwandte lebten. Auf dem Bau und als Pilzverkäufer für ein Delikatessengeschäft verdiente er sich etwas Geld. Er musste noch entnazifiziert werden. Mein Vater war nie Nazi, musste aber in die Partei, sonst hätte er in Leipzig keine Rechtsanwaltskanzlei aufmachen können. Sooft es ging, besuchte er uns schwarz. Er erzählte, dass er dabei grösseren Gefahren ausgesetzt war als im gesamten Krieg. Er wurde mit Hunden gehetzt und konnte sich nur durch den Polarstern in die richtige Richtung retten.

Da er als Rechtsanwalt auf der Sibirienliste für Zwangsarbeit stand, durfte niemand seinen Aufenthalt bemerken. Er kam meistens im Dunkeln mit einem bestimmten Vogelpfiff. Er konnte sich nie ankündigen. Um uns beim Holzsuchen zu helfen, zog er Mutters Kleider an. Grossvater wollte der hilfreichen 'Frau' fünf Mark geben, er hatte seinen Schwiegersohn nicht erkannt! Vater wurde immer einmal beim Grenzübergang geschnappt und konnte sich irgendwie befreien. Wenn es auf dem Weg zu uns geschah, brachte er keine Lebensmittel mit, die wurden ihm abgenommen. Durch eine fingierte Postkarte wussten wir, dass er gut zurückgekommen war. Eines Tages muss uns irgendjemand verpfiffen haben. Als die Kommission kam, versteckte sich mein Vater unter dem Schreibtisch. Da dieser hinten zu war und er sehr schlank, reichte der grosse Papierkorb zur Tarnung. Dies war der Auslöser, dass mein Vater versuchte, uns nach dem Westen zu holen.

Beim nächsten Besuch kam er mit Interzonenpass, er konnte in Bielefeld durch Unterstützung der Verwandten 'nachweisen', dass er schon vor dem Krieg dort gewohnt hatte. Meine kleine Schwester Andrea wurde darin eingetragen von uns, was keiner bemerkte. In Bielefeld angekommen, brach dann ihre Tuberkulose aus. Es begann eine sorgenvolle Zeit für die Eltern, aber Andrea war im Betheler Kinderkrankenhaus bestens versorgt.

Mit meiner Schwester Christel und mir ging meine Mutter 1950 jeweils einzeln schwarz über die Grenze in den Westen, bei Wolfenbüttel. Ich erinnere mich noch, wie wir von den Russen geschnappt wurden. Gleich nahm ich meinen Teddy und Hampelmann, die aus dem Rucksack schauten, in den Arm und weinte bitterlich. So liessen uns die kinderlieben Russen laufen. Es war ziemlicher Nebel und Mutter fand einen jungen

Burschen, der uns für Geld durch den Wald zur Grenze führte. Wir bekamen genaue Instruktionen, wann die Streife kam, und versteckten uns dann in einem Gebüsch. Als die Luft rein war, erreichten wir den freien Westen. In Hannover setzte meine Mutter mich in den Zug nach München, denn sie musste für den Umzug uns Kinder verteilen. Die Freunde von Grossmutter erwarteten mich, sie hatten eine weisse Kerze in der Hand und nahmen mich gleich lieb in den Arm. Zur Begrüssung bekam ich Nudeln, mein Lieblingsgericht. Durch den grossen Hunger ass ich ein halbes Pfund alleine, natürlich lag ich am nächsten Tag mit Bauchschmerzen im Bett. Aus vier Wochen wurde ein halbes Jahr.

Christel wurde mit unserer Mutter auch geschnappt, das war schwieriger, da Mutti einen langen Weg ohne Christel machen musste, die derweil bei den Volkspolizisten bleiben musste. Nach fünf Stunden bekam sie Christel wieder, die inzwischen gut verpflegt worden war und singend die Herren vergnügt hatte. Auch in dieser Nacht fand meine Mutter wieder Hilfe, um mit Christel schwarz die Grenze zu passieren. Sie kam nach Bayreuth zu Onkel und Tante. Bei den schwarzen Grenzübertritten hatten wir Kinder die Unterhosen voller silberner Bestecke.

Nachdem Vater nun ein Holzhaus gemietet hatte, sollte die Familie 1951 wieder vereint werden. Dieses Holzhaus aber war Schwarzbau, und da dort eine Strasse geplant war, musste das Haus abgerissen werden. Wir hätten nun nach Friedland ins Flüchtlingslager gemusst. Aber Grossvaters jüngste Schwester zog zu ihrer Tochter und überliess uns ihre Wohnung.

Wieder begann eine schwere Zeit für meine Eltern und ich muss sie wirklich bewundern, wie sie das alles geschafft haben. Die Wohnung war im Parterre, sie bestand aus einem grossen Zimmer mit dunkler weinroter Tapete. Dahinter war ein Wintergarten angebaut, deshalb mussten wir auch tagsüber im Zimmer immer Licht brennen. Es gab noch eine Familie und einen Journalisten in dieser Wohnung. Wir hatten für alle nur eine Toilette und eine Küche. Da wir kein fliessendes Wasser im Zimmer hatten, wuschen wir uns mit Schüssel und grosser Karaffe. Einmal wöchentlich gingen wir ins Volksbad. Christel schlief auf einem Sofa und ich im Feldbett im kalten Wintergarten und die Eltern in einem Bett. Ein Jahr lang spielte sich alles in dem Zimmer ab. Ich war leider alle Vierteljahre mit einer Mittelohrvereiterung geplagt, und bei meiner Mutter brach das schreckliche Gelenkrheuma aus.

Als unterernährte Kinder wurden wir beide erst mal nach Wangerooge geschickt. Dann kam ich in das Gymnasium, hatte aber in den Sprachen grosse Probleme. Mir fehlten in Englisch die Grundlagen, die ich nie richtig aufholte. Mit Andrea hatten wir grossen Kummer. Sie hatte lange Zeit Klinikaufenthalte und musste einige Operationen über sich ergehen lassen.

1952 bekamen wir eine Sozialwohnung am Rande von Bielefeld mit drei sehr kleinen Zimmerchen, aber wir hatten ein Bad und eine Küche und waren eine glückliche Familie. Später bekamen wir eine Bescheinigung zur legalen Übersiedlung nach Bielefeld, mit allen Möbeln aus Naunhof. Nur Silber und Markenporzellan durfte nicht ausgeführt werden. Nach zwei Jahren zogen wir wieder um in eine sehr schöne Dreizimmerwohnung im ersten Stock mit Garten. Allmählich ging es uns besser. Vater bekam eine kleine Handelsvertretung.

Aber Mutters Rheuma wurde immer schlimmer, und obwohl sie alle möglichen Kuren und Therapien versuchte, half eigentlich nichts. 1955 bestand ich die Mittlere Reife, und da Krankengymnastin mein Traumziel war, für die es aber eine Wartezeit von vier Jahren gab, entschied ich mich für die Ausbildung zur Medizinisch-technischen Assistentin.

Die Geborgenheit in der Familie hat mir stets Halt gegeben, um alle Ereignisse meiner Kindheit und Jugend gut zu überleben, wofür ich ewig dankbar bin.

Joachims Erinnerungen

An jenem vierten März 1945 lag die kleine Kreisstadt Greifenberg in Pommern (siehe Karte 10 für die wichtigsten im Text erwähnten Orte) schon seit Wochen tiefverschneit in winterlicher Ruhe. Eine trügerische Ruhe, die immer mehr zur ängstlichen Unruhe geworden war. Flüchtlingstrecks mit vielen Pferdewagen zogen durch die Königstrasse gen Westen und Militärkonvois in die umgekehrte Richtung nach Osten an die Front. Immer näher kam der Geschützdonner, zuerst nur ein entferntes Grummeln, das sich steigerte, bis schliesslich immer deutlicher die einzelnen Kanoneneinschläge zu hören waren. Nachts erschreckte uns Kinder das Blitzen dieses Granatfeuers, und wir verkrochen uns tief unter die Bettdecke.

An jenem vierten März 1945, einem Sonntag, wurde der Räumungsbefehl für Frauen und Kinder ausgerufen. So verliessen viele Greifenberger ihre Stadt, und auch wir gingen zum Bahnhof. Wir, das waren meine Mutter und ich, zehneinhalb Jahre alt, sowie drei Kinder einer Tante. Sie waren mit ihrer Mutter aus Königsberg in Ostpreussen geflohen. Ein Militärflugzeug brachte sie aus dem Kessel, stürzte aber durch einen Motorschaden bei Kolberg in Pommern ab. Während die Tante schwerverletzt im Krankenhaus lag, hatten wir die Kleinen zu uns genommen. Sie waren acht, sechs und drei Jahre alt.

Meine neunzehnjährige Schwester musste in Greifenberg bleiben. Dienstverpflichtet arbeitete sie bei der Post und durfte die Stadt nicht verlassen. Am Bahnhof herrschte ein grosses Durcheinander. Die Grossbahn transportierte nur noch Flüchtlinge, die aus dem Frontgebiet kamen, sowie Soldaten. Greifenberger wurden zur Kleinbahn verwiesen. Jeder von uns trug einen kleinen Rucksack, in dem das Notwendigste verstaut war. Die wenigen Personenwagen der Schmalspurbahn waren schon überfüllt. Wir kletterten in einen offenen Schüttgutwaggon, sassen dort frierend auf dem nackten Boden und warteten auf die Abfahrt.

Am Bahnsteig standen auch Schaulustige, die noch fest an den Endsieg glaubten. Ich erinnere mich an eine Bekannte, die meiner Mutter zurief: 'Was, Sie wollen auch fort? Wir bleiben hier! Heute früh wurde im Radio gesagt, dass der Führer jetzt seine Wunderwaffe einsetzt, und dann wird der Feind vernichtet!' - Was ist wohl aus dieser Frau geworden, als schon am nächsten Tage die Stadt in Flammen aufging und von der Roten Armee überrollt wurde? –

Es gab unzählige Tote unter der Zivilbevölkerung. Auch unser Familienkreis verlor sechs Angehörige. Der Jüngste war erst fünfzehn! - Wir jedoch hatten Glück! Unser Kleinbahnzug setzte sich schliesslich schnaubend in Bewegung. So nahmen wir Abschied von Greifenberg, noch nicht ahnend, dass es ein Abschied für immer war!

Bei heftigem Schneetreiben und Minusgraden kam unser Zug abends in Ziegenort an, einem Dorf am Stettiner Haff. Die Nacht verbrachten wir mit vielen anderen Flüchtlingen im Dorfkrug auf blanken Holzdielen. Am nächsten Morgen schipperte uns ein kleiner Dampfer ans andere Haffufer nach Stepenitz. Das wäre beinahe die letzte Fahrt gewesen! Ein russisches Kampfflugzeug nahm den Dampfer unter Beschuss, bis ein deutscher Jagdflieger den Feind angriff und abdrängte.

Von Stepenitz bis Stettin war es dann nicht mehr weit. Auf dem Hauptbahnhof wurden wir noch in einen völlig überfüllten

Zug gepfercht, Soldaten hoben uns Kinder durch die Fenster. Wir waren froh, schnell wieder aus der Stadt zu kommen, die fast jede Nacht bombardiert wurde.

Über Pasewalk, Neustrelitz, Wittenberge und Stendal erreichten wir nach Tagen endlich Tangermünde, unser Ziel. Hier lebten Verwandte, die uns erwarteten. Als kaufmännischer Direktor der Tangermünder Zucker- und Schokoladenfabriken bewohnte der Onkel mit seiner Familie eine geräumige Villa, in der auch wir ausreichend Platz hatten. Vierzehn Tage später kam auch meine Schwester an, die wir in Greifenberg zurücklassen mussten. Sie verliess die Stadt noch am selben Tag spät abends mit dem allerletzten Kleinbahnzug.

Nach weiteren zwei Wochen holte uns auch in Tangermünde der Krieg ein. Diesmal aber von Westen her. Amerikanische Truppen standen kurz vor der Stadt. Obwohl in Tangermünde bisher keine Bomben gefallen waren, in der Zuckerfabrik sollte englisches Kapital stecken, musste man jetzt doch mit Kampfhandlungen rechnen. Einige sogenannte 'Panzersperren' in den Strassen liessen das befürchten. Daher hatte die Fabrikdirektion Pferdewagen organisiert, die Frauen und Kinder für ein paar Tage in umliegende Dörfer bringen sollten, um dort in Sicherheit abzuwarten. Wir durften mitfahren.

Die erste Begegnung mit dem 'Feind' liess nicht lange auf sich warten. In einem Waldgebiet rollten plötzlich amerikanische Panzer auf unsere Wagenkolonne zu. Auf den Kettenfahrzeugen sassen gefangene deutsche Soldaten als lebende Schutzschilde! Ganz schön clever, diese Amis! Wer würde schon auf die eigenen Kameraden schiessen! Wir wurden nicht überrollt und kamen schliesslich in ein nahegelegenes Dorf, in dem man uns in Scheunen Unterschlupf gewährte.

Auf dem Kirchturm hielt ein Bauer Ausguck und beobachtete mit einem Fernglas die Landstrasse. Wenn sich feindliche Einheiten näherten, hängte er ein weisses Bettlaken aus dem Turmfenster als Zeichen der Kapitulation. Kamen dagegen deutsche Truppen, wurde das Laken schnell eingeholt und gegen eine Hakenkreuzfahne ausgewechselt. Auf Kapitulation stand schliesslich die Todesstrafe, und die deutschen Feldjäger, auch Kettenhunde genannt, kannten kein Erbarmen. Sie knüpften so manchen am nächsten Laternenpfahl auf! Daher erfolgte an diesem Tage mehrmals ein Flaggenwechsel auf dem Kirchturm!

Boten brachten schliesslich die Nachricht, dass wir wieder zurückfahren sollten. Amerikanische Truppen hatten Tangermünde eingenommen. Als unsere Pferdewagen in die Stadt fuhren, wurden wir von Passanten mit Bonbons beworfen. Die Schokoladenfabrik war geplündert worden. Viele Anwohner hatten sich reichlich mit Süssigkeiten, Zucker und Aromata eingedeckt. Begehrte Tauschobjekte! Wir Kinder liebten vor allem die Nährstangen, eine Tangermünder Spezialität. Sie gibt es dort sogar heute noch zu kaufen!

In Tangermünde hatte es zum Glück keine nennenswerten Gefechte gegeben. Nachdem die deutschen Truppen sich über die Elbe nach Osten abgesetzt und die Brücke in die Luft gesprengt hatten, leisteten die wenigen Volkssturm-Rentner, die in der Stadt verblieben waren, den einrückenden Amerikanern keinen Widerstand mehr. Nur ein paar fanatische Hitlerjungen, halbe Kinder noch, mussten unbedingt Helden spielen. Aus einem Kellerfenster schossen sie mit einer

Panzerfaust auf vorbeifahrende Kettenfahrzeuge. Die Burschen wurden schnell gefasst und erbarmungslos erschossen!

Wir hatten uns gerade wieder in der Villa des Onkels eingerichtet, da erging ein Räumungsbefehl der amerikanischen Kommandantur. Alle Einwohner mussten die Stadt verlassen. Keiner wusste warum! Auch wir zogen in das 7 km entfernte Dorf Heeren. Dort waren schon etwa 6000 Tangermünder, ein dichtes Gewimmel! Auf dem Bauernhof, auf dem wir einquartiert wurden, tummelten sich über 130 Leute. Fast eine Woche verging, bevor alle wieder in die Stadt zurück durften.

Viele Häuser und Wohnungen waren geplündert und verwüstet. In der Zuckerfabrik hatten sich Gefangenenlager mit Russen und Polen befunden, die dort arbeiten mussten. Diese nun Befreiten hatten die Gelegenheit genutzt und sich für ihre Zwangsarbeit entschädigt! Reguläre Besatzer waren wohl auch involviert. Ich sah einen farbigen Amerikaner, der an jedem Unterarm mindestens fünf Armbanduhren trug, die er stolz zeigte! In der Villa des Onkels befand sich inzwischen ein amerikanisches Lazarett. So mussten wir uns eine andere Bleibe suchen.

Nach einiger Zeit zogen die Amerikaner ab. Kanadische Einheiten kamen, die schliesslich durch britische Truppen abgelöst wurden.

In Jalta hatten Deutschlands Gegner vereinbart, dass die alliierten Westmächte nur bis zur Elbe vorrücken sollten. Von Osten her musste die Rote Armee die Front aufrollen und bis zur Elbe marschieren. Daher warteten die Engländer in Tangermünde die Zeit ab. Nachmittags, zum 'five-o-clock-tea' fuhren ihre Panzer auf den Weinberg und schossen etwa eine halbe Stunde lang über die Elbe hinüber auf die dort noch befindlichen deutschen Einheiten. Diese leisteten jedoch keine Gegenwehr mehr und zogen sich von den Wiesen in die Wälder zurück. Schliesslich gab es eines Tages einen peinlichen Zwischenfall. Wieder einmal schossen die Tommies, wie wir die Engländer nannten, nach drüben auf dort fahrende Militärfahrzeuge. Es waren aber keine Deutschen, sondern Russen, die das gar nicht schön fanden und erbost zurückballerten. Sorry, so etwas konnte schon mal in der Hitze des Gefechts passieren! Übrigens waren das die letzten Schüsse dieses Krieges in Tangermünde!

In Jalta wurde auch beschlossen, dass die Alliierten grössere Gebiete auf der Westseite der Elbe an die sowjetische Besatzungsmacht abgeben mussten. Dafür durften die Westmächte in Berlin einrücken. Die deutsche Hauptstadt, die von der Roten Armee erobert worden war, wurde so zur Vier-Sektoren-Stadt.

Für Tangermünde hiess das nochmals einen Wechsel der Besatzer. Die Engländer zogen ab, und die Russen übernahmen die Stadt. Wir Deutschen waren darüber nicht glücklich. Vor allem Frauen mussten nun aufpassen. Immer wieder kam es zu Vergewaltigungen, obwohl Offiziere manchmal hart durchgriffen und die Strolche bestraften. Ich habe selbst mit angesehen, wie ein Muschkote, so hiessen die einfachen russischen Soldaten bei uns, von einem Vorgesetzten krankenhausreif geprügelt wurde!

Für Tangermünder Jungs begann eine aufregende Zeit. Neben der alten gesprengten Elbbrücke bauten die Russen eine neue aus Holz. Auch Deutsche durften sie passieren. So zog es uns nach der Schule immer auf die andere Elbseite hinüber. Dort hatte die deutsche Wehrmacht massenhaft Kriegsgerät und Munition hinterlassen. Es war zwar streng untersagt, so etwas anzufassen oder gar damit zu spielen, aber wer hielt sich schon an dieses Verbot? Mit Handgranaten, die in Seen und Teiche geworfen wurden, liessen sich viele Fische erbeuten. Eine willkommene Bereicherung des sonst so dürftigen Speiseplans!

Das Schiessen mit Karabinern fanden wir nicht so toll, da es durch den Rückstoss des abgefeuerten Gewehres oft blaue Flecken an den Schultern gab. Mit Pistolen dagegen wurde so manches Wettschiessen veranstaltet! Schwarzpulver liess sich für viele Zwecke einsetzen und war sehr begehrt. Wir holten es aus Granathülsen, deren Sprengköpfe kunstgerecht abgehebelt wurden. In Schülerranzen versteckt, schmuggelten wir die Konterbande grinsend an den russischen Posten auf der Elbbrücke vorbei. Dass dieses gefährliche Treiben auch schiefgehen konnte, war abzusehen. Einige Schüler verletzten sich schwer, einer kam sogar ums Leben. Schliesslich hörte der makabre Zeitvertreib auf. Die Vernunft siegte auch bei den mutigsten Draufgängern!

Das grösste Problem dieser Zeit war der allgegenwärtige Hunger. Die mageren Rationen, die es auf Lebensmittelkarten gab, reichten nicht aus, um heranwachsende Kinder satt zu machen. So ging man oft mit knurrendem Magen zu Bett. An meinem elften Geburtstag hatte ich nur einen Wunsch: Mich einmal so richtig am Brot satt zu essen! Selbsthilfe war angesagt! Auf abgeernteten Feldern wurden Kornähren gesammelt und übriggebliebene Kartoffeln gerodet. Aus Löwenzahn-, Brennnessel- und Sauerampferblättern entstanden schmackhafte Salate und Suppen.

Dann gab es noch die illegale Nahrungsbeschaffung: In Obstplantagen stibitzten wir Beeren, Birnen und Äpfel. Dabei musste man sehr aufpassen, nicht vom Feldhüter erwischt zu werden. Sie verprügelten Erntediebe gnadenlos! Im Herbst wurden tonnenweise Zuckerrüben zur Verarbeitung in die Fabriken gebracht. Viele Wagen fuhren durch die Strassen, hochaufgeschüttet voller Rüben. Das weckte natürlich Begehrlichkeiten! Die sportlichsten von uns sprangen hinten an die Hänger, klammerten sich dort mit einer Hand fest und mit der anderen warfen sie so viel vom Wagen herunter, wie sie greifen konnten, bis die Puste ausging. Das Fussvolk sammelte die Beute auf. Alles musste blitzschnell gehen, damit der Fahrer nichts bemerkte. Zu Hause fragten die Mütter nicht, woher die Rüben kamen. Sie wurden stillschweigend verarbeitet.

Als der Winter vor der Tür stand, er wurde 1945-46 sehr, sehr kalt, musste für genügend Heizungsmaterial vorgesorgt werden. Die wenigen Kohlenzuteilungen reichten bei weitem nicht aus, um immer eine warme Stube zu haben. In den umliegenden Wäldern waren viele emsig damit beschäftigt, Säcke mit Kienäppeln voll zu stopfen. Alles herumliegende Astholz wurde aufgesammelt, man rodete Baumstubben in mühevoller Handarbeit und fällte auch so manch dünnes Bäumchen, wenn der Förster mal nicht aufpasste. Der Wald sah danach wie gefegt aus! Auf dem Reichsbahngelände lagerten Kohlenberge. Sie wurden von Russen bewacht. Hier liessen wir Jungs uns auch etwas einfallen. Mädchen wurden als Lockvögel vorgeschickt. Sie gingen zu den Wachposten, schäkerten mit ihnen herum und lenkten sie ab. Das war dann der Moment, wo wir uns von der anderen Seite anschlichen und schnell ein paar Briketts klauten. Not macht erfinderisch!

Langsam normalisierte sich das Leben wieder. Unser Vater, der als Soldat in Dänemark stationiert gewesen war, wurde Ende 1946 aus englischer Kriegsgefangenschaft entlassen und kam zu uns. So war die Familie wieder glücklich vereint!

Nach der Schulzeit gingen für mich auch die Jahre in Tangermünde zu Ende. Berufliche Orientierungen erforderten Ortswechsel, bis ich schliesslich 1960 in Berlin meine neue Heimat fand.

Gerne denke ich noch an die schöne alte Kaiserstadt an der Elbe zurück, die mir zur zweiten Heimat wurde, nachdem die erste verlorenging. Für jeden mag der Begriff 'Heimat' eine eigene Bedeutung haben. Die Älteren sehen darin nur den Ort, wo sie geboren und aufgewachsen sind. Dazu gehörten auch meine Eltern. Sie wurden in Tangermünde nicht heimisch und konnten sich nicht damit abfinden, dass sie aus ihrem geliebten Greifenberg in Pommern für immer vertrieben wurden, dort wo seit mehr als siebenhundert Jahren ihre deutschen Vorfahren gelebt hatten. Die Jüngeren definieren das Wort 'Heimat' grosszügiger. Für sie ist Heimat überall dort, wo sie sich wohlfühlen, wo sie glücklich und geborgen sind. Zu denen gehöre auch ich!

Renates Erinnerungen

Als ich 1938 als zweites Kind meiner Eltern – mein Bruder war gerade ein Jahr alt – in einem südöstlichen Vorort von Berlin (siehe Karte 11 für die wichtigsten im Text erwähnten Orte) geboren wurde, war noch nicht Krieg, aber es war in Deutschland auch nicht Frieden. Trotzdem waren die ersten Jahre meines Lebens behütet und unbeschwert. Wir spielten in unserem kleinen Garten, und mein Bruder und ich waren unzertrennlich wie Zwillinge.

Meine Eltern waren keine Anhänger von Hitler geschweige denn Nazis – mein Vater stammte aus einer kinderreichen, sozialdemokratischen Arbeiterfamilie und hatte sich zum Studienrat für Englisch und Deutsch hochgearbeitet – aber sie waren auch nicht im Widerstand: was für ein Held hätte man mit zwei, später drei kleinen Kindern sein müssen?

1941 wurde mein Vater an das Goethe-Gymnasium in Landsberg an der Warthe – das ist jenseits der Oder, heute Gorzow in Polen – versetzt und 1943 von dort schliesslich an die Kriegsfront im Westen eingezogen. 1944 wurde meine Schwester als sogenanntes 'Fronturlaubskind' bei Fliegeralarm geboren. Sie musste schon als frisch geborener Säugling hungern, weil meine Mutter ganz abgemagert war. Dennoch hatten wir Glück: Im Januar 1945, die Russische Armee war schon so nahe, dass man die Geschütze hören konnte, wurden wir von einem Nachbarn mit dem Lastwagen nach Berlin mitgenommen – meine Mutter, wir drei Kinder, damals sieben und sechs Jahre und 10 Monate alt, und mein 80jähriger Grossvater - mit nichts als dem nackten Leben. Ich erinnere mich nicht mehr, aber zu der Zeit muss es noch Brücken über die Oder gegeben haben, die später gesprengt wurden. Wohl aber erinnere ich mich an brennende Panzer und Tote am Wegesrand.

In Berlin angekommen, krochen wir zunächst bei meiner Grossmutter im Stadtteil Wedding in der grossen Wohnung im vierten Stock eines Berliner Mietshauses unter. Da war es richtig eng, ausser uns hatten zahlreiche Tanten und Cousins und Cousinen aus der grossen Familie meines Vaters ebenfalls dort Unterschlupf gesucht.

Wenn man die Wahrheit über den Stand der Kriegsfronten wissen wollte, musste man den sogenannten BumBum-Sender im Radio suchen (was natürlich strengstens verboten war), das war die BBC, die auf ständig wechselnden Frequenzen sendete und über den Anfang der Fünften Sinfonie von Beethoven zu erkennen war: Ta-ta-ta-taaaa… Da hörte meine Mutter dann, wie es um den Krieg wirklich stand.

In Berlin tobte im Frühjahr 1945 der Luftkampf, jede Nacht wurden wir aus dem Schlaf gerissen und in den Luftschutzkeller gebracht, kahle graue Räume, in denen wir verängstigt sassen und die Einschläge der Bomben in der Nähe hörten und spürten. Noch heute kann ich keine Sirene hören, ohne an Bomben und Luftschutzkeller zu denken. Eines Nachts wurde die Vorderfront unseres Hauses weggebombt, auch das Schlafzimmer meiner Grossmutter, die daraufhin die Tür zum Schlafzimmer verrammelte, damit nicht jemand ins Freie treten und vier Stockwerke in die Tiefe stürzen konnte. Wir konnten aber wegen des Platzmangels nicht mehr dort bleiben und mussten zu Verwandten meiner Mutter in eine Villa im ehemals vornehmen Vorort Schlachtensee weiter ziehen. Das waren noch immer wohlhabende Leute, die sich dann als 'Miete' die Lebensmittelkarten von uns Kindern für ihren eigenen einzigen Sohn geben liessen. In der Not lernt man Menschen kennen! Mein Vater hat nach dem Krieg die Verbindung zu diesen Verwandten abgebrochen.

In Schlachtensee erlebten wir den Endkampf um Berlin, erst kamen die Russen, dann die Amerikaner. Zwei Erinnerungen habe ich daran ganz deutlich. Einmal hatten einfache russische Soldaten auf der Suche nach Uhren und Schmuck uns alle schon bei vorgehaltener Maschinenpistole an die Wand gestellt, als ein russischer Offizier dazu kam, der freundlich und kinderlieb war und der Bedrohung ein Ende machte. Er schenkte uns sogar noch Kekse! Das war für uns halb verhungerte Kinder mit rachitischen Bäuchen eine Sensation, denn zu der Zeit ernährten wir uns z.B. von Brennnessel'spinat' und Kartoffelschalen, die meine Mutter aus fremden Mülleimern sammelte und zu einer Art Puffer verarbeitete. Demgegenüber erinnere ich mich an einen Vorfall, als die Amerikaner dann in der Nachbarvilla einquartiert waren. Ein baumlanger schwarzer Amerikaner schüttete hinter dem Zaun seine Bohnensuppe aus dem Kochgeschirr vor meinen ausgehungerten 'Nazikind'-Augen demonstrativ in den Sand. Propaganda wirkt eben überall, so wie ich – auch als Ergebnis von Kriegspropaganda – noch Jahre nach dem Krieg träumte, ich sässe auf der Kellertreppe und die Russen kämen und hackten mich in Stücke.

Meine Mutter hat später erzählt, wie sie einmal mit Hunden vom Hof gejagt wurde, als sie versuchte, ihr letztes 'schönes' Kleid bei Bauern im Berliner Umland gegen etwas Essbares zu tauschen. Die Bauern hatten damals bereits viele eingetauschte Wertgegenstände gehortet, und wir hatten eben nichts. Meine Mutter hat mir dann sogar erzählt, dass ihr fast die Augen aus dem Kopf gefallen wären, als die Bäuerin den Hunden Fleisch in den Fressnapf geschüttet hat.

1945/46 war ein besonders kalter Winter, wir bekamen kein Brennmaterial, und meine Geschwister und ich hatten dicke Frostbeulen an Händen und Füssen. Von der Kirche hatten wir gebrauchte Schuhe bekommen, in die wir dann aber nicht hinein passten. Es wurden Lappen um die Füsse gewickelt, und irgendwo hatte meine Mutter Kampfersalbe organisiert, die ein wenig half.

Wir erlebten die Teilung Berlins in vier Sektoren, die den vier Siegermächten USA, Russland, Grossbritannien und Frankreich zugeteilt wurden. Es war ein glücklicher Zufall, dass wir uns in einem Stadtteil befanden, der dann zu Westberlin gehörte. Ein weiterer Glücksfall war, dass mein Vater in britische Kriegsgefangenschaft geraten war, wo er als Dolmetscher arbeiten konnte. 1947 kam er nach Hause, meine kleine Schwester, die ihn gar nicht kannte, sagte „guck mal, da kommt Onkel Willi", als unser Vater durch die Tür trat. Da er kein NS-Mitglied gewesen und unbelastet war, wurde er wieder in den Schuldienst aufgenommen.

Wir erlebten die Währungsreform und im Kalten Krieg die Blockade Berlins durch die Russen, die die Westmächte mit einer Luftbrücke durchbrachen, wobei unter den Piloten auch Opfer zu beklagen waren. Die Berliner nannten diese Flugzeuge liebevoll „Rosinenbomber", weil sie Lebensmittelpakete abwarfen. Wenn ich die Augen schliesse, kann ich die Trockenmöhren und Pom, den Kartoffelbrei, noch heute schmecken. Das Luftbrückendenkmal, das die Stadt Berlin später den Piloten und den Opfern am ehemaligen Flughafen Tempelhof errichtet hat und das von den Berlinern wegen seiner gabelartigen Form 'Hungerharke' genannt wird, erinnert noch heute an diese Zeit.

Wir bekamen wieder eine eigene Wohnung, Schulunterricht begann. Mein Bruder und ich wurden gleich in die zweite bzw. dritte Klasse aufgenommen, da meine Mutter uns während der letzten Phase des Krieges und danach selbst unterrichtet hatte. Wir konnten zwar lesen, schreiben und rechnen, aber wir waren ebenso wie die meisten anderen Kinder verstört und taten Dinge, die wir ohne den Krieg sicher nie getan hätten. Ich erinnere mich, dass ich in der Schule einmal ein blau-buntes Chiffontuch fand, das ich natürlich nicht hätte mitnehmen dürfen. Aber ich nahm es mit nach Hause, weil ich so sehr gern meiner Mutter eine Freude machen wollte. Natürlich wurde ich befragt und musste das Tuch am nächsten Tag zurück bringen. War ich nun eine Diebin?

Mein Vater rauchte Pfeife, deshalb zog er auf dem Balkon Tabak, aber auch Tomaten. Wir Kinder sammelten Pferdeäpfel als Dünger (5 Pfennige Lohn für den Eimer). Kienäpfel wurden für den Ofen gesammelt, manchmal hatte man Glück und konnte hinter einem Kohlenlaster etwas Kohlenstaub auffegen.

Durch die Freundschaft meines Vaters zu Professor Harold Picton, bei dem er vor dem Krieg in London studiert hatte, bekam ich eine englische Brieffreundin für meine ersten Versuche mit der englischen Sprache. Als mein Vater 1953 Direktor an einem Gymnasium wurde, hatte seine Schule eine Partnerschaft mit Nunthorpe Grammar School in York und wir bekamen Austauschschüler von dort. Die englischen Bücher aus der Bibliothek meines Vaters haben mich mein Leben lang begleitet.

Das deutsche Wirtschaftswunder begann. Meine Eltern mussten allerdings bei null anfangen, und ich habe noch mehrere Jahre nach dem Krieg nur geerbte und von meiner Mutter geänderte Kleidung getragen. Manchmal habe ich mich dafür geschämt, wenn Klassenkameradinnen mich mit meinen unmodischen Sachen aufzogen. Aber langsam ging es voran, ich schloss die Schule 1956 mit 17 Jahren mit dem Abitur ab und konnte eine Ausbildung an der Fachschule machen. 1958 begann ich zu arbeiten.

In Deutschland begann endlich auch die Aufarbeitung des Naziregimes. Ich erinnere mich nicht, dass wir im Schulunterricht das sogenannte Dritte Reich behandelt hätten. Irgendwie endete Historie immer bei Napoleon und Bismarck. Die Nürnberger Prozesse habe ich noch nicht bewusst miterlebt, und in der Bevölkerung wurde die NS-Zeit eisern verdrängt und tot geschwiegen, alle waren mit dem Wiederaufbau (ich möchte hoffen, auch mit Schock und Scham?) beschäftigt. Aber zu Beginn der 60er Jahre gab es die ersten Prozesse gegen NS-Verbrecher, und was in den Zeitungen darüber berichtet wurde, erschien mir ganz unvorstellbar. Da begann ich mich umzublicken und zu fragen 'der oder der oder die...?' Was haben sie getan, was wussten sie, was hätten sie wissen können/müssen? Der Blick auf meine Kindheit weitete sich vom Kriegsschrecken mit Hungern, Frieren und Angst, Angst, Angst auf die Schuld unseres Volkes, ich kämpfte mit meinem Selbstverständnis als Deutsche, Scham und Schuldgefühle sind oft noch immer präsent.

Rolfs Erinnerungen

Ich wurde 1937 in München (siehe Karte 12 für die wichtigsten im Text erwähnten Orte) geboren und bald darauf zogen wir nach Starnberg in Bayern um. Als ich ungefähr vier oder fünf Jahre alt war, fuhr meine Mutter mit mir nach Berlin, um ihre Schwester zu besuchen. Eine meiner ersten Erinnerungen war ein Grossangriff auf Berlin. Wir verbrachten unsere erste und einzige Nacht in Berlin im Keller. Am nächsten Morgen brachen wir sofort auf, um nach Hause zu fahren. Wir gingen zum Bahnhof durch Strassen, die wie Schuttkegel zwischen den stehengebliebenen Häuserfassaden aussahen. Die gröbsten Brocken lagen in der Mitte der Strasse, die selbst nicht mehr sichtbar war. Weiter oben lagen die kleineren Brocken der zerstörten Mauerwerke. So sind wir den langen Weg durch diese gespenstische Landschaft der Zerstörung zum Bahnhof gegangen.

Als ich in die Schule kam, wurde erwartet, dass wir Schüler mit dem deutschen 'Führergruss' den Schultag beginnen. Da ich offensichtlich nicht im 'richtigen Geist' erzogen worden war, hob ich den falschen, linken Arm zum Gruss. Das hätte bei linientreuen Nazi-Lehrern Rückschlüsse auf eine nicht linienkonforme Familie und damit Ärger geben können. Zum Glück hat mein Lehrer das übersehen und es hatte keine Folgen.

Als Starnberg unter einem Bombenangriff mit vielen Opfern litt, beschloss meine Mutter, in unser Haus nach Eichstätt im Altmühltal umzuziehen. Die Stadt schien von Luftangriffen verschont zu bleiben, da dort ein Gefangenenlager für englische Offiziere war. In Eichstätt war der Textilbetrieb meines Vaters, der kein Parteimitglied war und der noch vor

Beginn des Krieges zum Einmarsch in Österreich zum Militär eingezogen worden war. Der Betrieb musste auf Uniformherstellung umgestellt werden und wurde gleich einem Betriebsleiter anvertraut, der ein Parteimitglied war und der sich später, als mein Vater lange in französischer Kriegsgefangenschaft war, den Textilbetrieb aneignete.

Meine Mutter hörte regelmässig BBC im Radio. Die Nutzung dieser beliebten Informationsquelle, angekündigt durch die bekannte da-da-da dam (Beethoven) – Melodie war aber riskant und hätte die Todesstrafe nach sich ziehen können. Zur Nachrichtenzeit wurde daher unser Schäferhund in den grossen Garten gelassen und da unser Haus als letztes oben am Berg lag, hätte er uns vor jedem Mithörer gewarnt.

Von dieser Position oberhalb des Altmühltales, konnten wir die alliierten Bombergeschwader sehr gut beobachten, die im Sommer 1944 in ungeheurer Zahl in Richtung München zogen. Sie flogen in Formationen von viermal vier ungefähr zwei stundenlang fast jeden Tag über uns hinweg. Diese silberglänzenden Bomber am blauen Himmel habe ich noch heute lebhaft vor Augen.

An einem der letzten Kriegstage sollten die gefangenen, englischen Offiziere verlegt werden. Die offensichtlich hervorragende Information der Alliierten besagte, dass das Gefangenenlager frühmorgens um sieben Uhr geräumt werden sollte. Aber Verzögerungen führten zum verspäteten Abmarsch der Kriegsgefangenen. Tiefflieger entdeckten die Marschkolonnen und beschossen sie, nicht ahnend, dass sie damit hunderte ihrer eigenen Leute umbrachten.

Von unserem Haus hatten wir auch einen guten Blick auf eine Altmühlbrücke und die zu ihr führende Allee. Die Brücke wurde am letzten Kriegstag gesprengt und wir konnten beobachten, wie die amerikanischen Panzer zwar langsam, aber ohne Schwierigkeiten den flachen Fluss auf den Trümmern der Brücke überquerten. An den Bäumen der Allee waren von der SS auch noch zwei Eichstätter aufgehängt worden, die ein paar Stunden zu früh weisse Fahnen aus den Fenstern gehängt hatten.

Unser Haus wurde sofort von Amerikanern beschlagnahmt und wir trugen das Nötigste zu freundlichen Nachbarn, die uns aufnahmen. Aber nach einigen Tagen durften wir schon wieder in das Souterrain unseres Hauses einziehen. Meine Mutter wurde zum Übersetzen und Kaffeekochen herangeholt. Ab und zu fiel auch für uns etwas vom Essen ab und da wir unseren Garten weiter bearbeiten durften, hatten wir keine Hungersnot. Auch hatten wir Hühner, deren Eier sehr von den Amerikanern geschätzt wurden. Ein schwarzer Soldat, 'Soapy', tauschte bei uns gerne frische Eier gegen Konserven und Schokolade. Ihm verdanke ich auch meine erste Banane.

Als es eines Abends klingelte, musste meine Mutter die Tür öffnen, wobei hinter ihr gleich mehrere „unserer" Amerikaner mit gezogener Pistole standen, da sie immer noch bewaffnete Deutsche auf der Flucht befürchteten. Aber es war nur ein ‚Fräulein', der es zu langweilig geworden war, im Auto auf ihren amerikanischen Freund zu warten.

Als bei meinem Vater - zu der Zeit in Russland - das Ende des Krieges abzusehen war, machte er sich in Richtung Westen auf, mit dem Ziel, in die amerikanische Gefangenschaft zu kommen. Das gelang ihm nach ungefähr vierzehn Tagen

Nachtwanderung, aber er wurde von den Amerikanern gleich an die Franzosen ausgeliefert. Dort musste er schwere Waldarbeit bei minimaler Ernährung verrichten. Nach Auflösung des Kriegsgefangenenlagers blieb er in Frankreich. Meine Eltern waren dann schon geschieden und er heiratete dort später eine Französin. So sah ich ihn erst mit 15 Jahren wieder und dabei und auch bei den späteren, seltenen Treffen haben wir nie über die Kriegsgeschehen gesprochen.

Roswithas Erinnerungen

Ich wurde am 26. Dezember 1937 in Eichberg, bei Bunzlau in Schlesien (siehe Karte 13 für die wichtigsten im Text erwähnten Orte) geboren. Da ich ein sechs-Monatskind bin, war es für meine Mutter eine Höchstleistung, mich im Winter 1937 durchzubringen. Die nächste Kinderklinik mit den notwendigen Apparaturen für ein 'Frühchen' mit 1300 Gramm Gewicht bei der Geburt war im strengen Winter 1937 nicht erreichbar. Da meine Mutter zu diesem Zeitpunkt auch in keiner Weise mit meiner Geburt gerechnet hatte, gab es also auch weder Kinderkleidung noch andere Hilfsmittel wie z.B. Trinkfläschchen oder dergleichen in unserem Haushalt. Wir, d.h. meine Eltern, mein zwei-einhalb Jahre älterer Bruder und ich, wuchsen auf dem Gut der Grosseltern väterlicherseits auf. Mein Vater fuhr in die nächstgelegene Kreisstadt, kaufte Babysachen und eine Spielzeug-Trinkflasche, mit der mir meine Mutter – sobald ich wach war – tropfenweise Nahrung zuführte.

Ich habe also trotz der Frühgeburt eine normale Kindheit auf dem Gut verbracht. Schon mit fünf Jahren wurde ich in die Dorfschule eingeschult, da ich dabei ertappt wurde, wie ich mich mit den Schularbeiten meines Bruders beschäftigte. In der Dorfschule waren jeweils drei Jahrgänge zusammengefasst. Bald wurde der Unterricht immer sporadischer, der Lehrer aus dem Nachbarort hatte den Unterricht übernommen, dann fiel er gänzlich aus, als der Lehrer eingezogen wurde.

Bis zu diesem Zeitpunkt haben wir im Grunde nichts weiter vom Kriegsgeschehen mitbekommen. Als die ersten Flüchtlinge aus weiter östlich gelegenen Gebieten bei uns durchzogen und auch mein Vater zum Militärdienst eingezogen wurde, erlebten wir Veränderungen, die der Krieg mit sich brachte.

Im Februar 1945 ging meine Mutter mit uns Kindern und ihren Schwiegereltern mit drei Gespannen auf die Flucht. Am zweiten Tag verstarb meine Grossmutter an einer Lungenembolie. Es war meine erste unmittelbare Begegnung mit dem Tod. Nach der Beerdigung ging unsere Flucht weiter. Wir sind nicht mit dem grossen Treck gefahren, hielten uns immer mehr oder weniger auf uns selbst gestützt und auf den grossen Bekanntenkreis meines Grossvaters. Überall fanden wir eine Unterkunft für die Tiere und uns, bis die Maul- und Klauenseuche unsere Fahrt in Hoyerswerda nordöstlich von Dresden unterbrach. Nach sechs Wochen des Wartens darauf, dass die Tiere vom Veterinäramt für die Weiterfahrt freigegeben werden, fuhren wir weiter Richtung Brandenburg, wo ein Vetter meines Grossvaters ein Grossgut mit seiner Frau besass. Mein Grossvater war der Meinung, dass uns dort nichts fehlen könnte. Dass uns die Russische Armee auch dort einholen könnte, hatte er nicht erwartet. Aber so geschah es im April 1945. Meiner Mutter war allerdings der Aufenthalt auf dem Lande zu unsicher. Sie zog deshalb mit meinem Bruder und mir in die nächste Kreisstadt: Wittsock an der Dosse. Dort lebte eine Cousine meines Vaters, die uns auch bei sich aufnahm. Hier hatte ich ein besonderes Erlebnis:

Die Cousine meines Vaters besass eine Plantage mit schwarzen Johannesbeeren. Meine Mutter half mit meinem Bruder und mir beim Beeren pflücken. Eines Tages hatte ich dabei mit meinem Bruder Streit bekommen, so dass ich schliesslich in Tränen ausbrach. In diesem Augenblick kam ein russischer Besatzungssoldat auf uns zu, gab uns zu verstehen, dass wir auf ihn warten sollten. Nach kurzer Zeit kam er zurück und überreichte mir ein ganzes Kommissbrot, strich mir über den Kopf dabei und deutete meinem Bruder an, nicht wieder mit mir in Streit zu geraten. Dann ging er weiter. Meine Mutter, die die Szene beobachtet hatte, kam zu uns und freudestrahlend gab ich ihr das Brot.

Die russischen Soldaten galten durchweg als sehr kinderfreundlich; nur die Mongolen waren bei uns Kindern nicht beliebt: vielleicht lag es an den Schlitzaugen, die uns verängstigten. Ich habe aber niemals eine direkte Begegnung mit ihnen gehabt.

Von meinem Vater hatten wir seit dem Winter 1944 nichts mehr gehört. Meine Mutter hat ihm aber laufend von der Flucht berichtet. Sie schrieb immer offene Postkarten an seine Feldpostnummer.

Im August 1945 wurden die Schulen in der damaligen Sowjetischen Besatzungszone wieder geöffnet und ich kam in die dritte Klasse. Im September 1945 vertraute meine Mutter meinem Bruder und mir an, dass sie mit uns nachts einen Fluchtversuch über die „Ohre", einen Nebenfluss der Elbe, nach Niedersachsen wagen wollte. Und so kam es, dass wir drei Ende September „schwarz" über die Grenze in den von den Westmächten besetzten Teil Deutschlands kamen. Mein Grossvater kam nicht mit, er hatte immer noch die Hoffnung, eines Tages wieder nach Schlesien zurückzukehren. So schrieb er auch bis zu seinem Tod im Jahr 1953 seinen Absender immer mit dem Hinweis „ z.Zt".

Nach acht Tagen, in denen meine Mutter, mein Bruder und ich durch verschiedene Lager in Hamburg geschleust wurden, erreichten wir meine Grosseltern mütterlicherseits, bepackt mit einem kleinen Rucksack. Wir waren mit drei Gespannen und unserem ganzen Hab und Gut auf die Flucht gegangen. Was uns geblieben war, passte nun in einen Rucksack.

Aber das Schönste war, dass acht Tage nach uns mein Vater aus russischer Gefangenschaft in Hamburg eintraf. Er hatte sich gedacht, dass wir bei seinen Schwiegereltern gelandet sein würden. Übrigens, die Feldpostkarten hatten ihn erreicht: so wusste er, dass seine Mutter auf der Flucht verstorben war und es für ihn kein Schlesien mehr gab.

Acknowledgements

First and foremost we would like to thank all of our friends who wrote down their memories for this book. We had all wanted to, indeed needed to write down these stories to confront our long forgotten memories of that time, but it took a concerted and communal decision to actually do it while we still could.

Next, our thanks go out to all of our friends for their continuing interest, support and encouragement. We are particularly grateful to our families, children and grandchildren for their searching questions which helped us to bring this work to fruition.

Finally, we are above all indebted to Margaret, Jim and Genevieve for carefully going through the manuscripts correcting and proof-reading them. All remaining mistakes are entirely our own.

Danksagungen

Zuerst und vor allem möchten wir allen unseren Freundinnen und Freunden danken, die ihre Erinnerungen für dieses Buch aufgeschrieben haben. Wir hatten alle den Wunsch, ja das Bedürfnis, diese Geschichten aufzuschreiben, um uns mit den lange verdrängten Erinnerungen aus jener Zeit auseinander zu setzen, aber es brauchte diese konzertierte, gemeinsame Entscheidung, es zu tun, solange wir noch können.

Weiterhin danken wir all unseren Freunden für ihr andauerndes Interesse, ihre Unterstützung und Ermutigung. Besonders sind wir auch unseren Familien, Kindern und Enkelkindern für ihre kritischen Nachfragen dankbar, die zum Gelingen dieser Arbeit beitrugen.

Schließlich schulden wir vor allem Margaret, Jim und Genevieve Dank für das sorgfältige Durchsehen der Manuskripte, für Verbesserungs-vorschläge und Korrekturen. Für alle verbliebenen Fehler sind allein wir verantwortlich.

Printed in Great Britain
by Amazon.co.uk, Ltd.,
Marston Gate.